R-4200-A

The Rise and Fall of National Security Decisionmaking in the Former USSR

Implications for Russia and the Commonwealth

Harry Gelman

Prepared for the
United States Army

RAND

Approved for public release; distribution unlimited

PREFACE

This study examines the political-military mechanisms used in the Soviet Union in the Gorbachev era for national security decisionmaking, and explains how the struggle over control of those mechanisms contributed to the events that led to the failed coup of August 1991. The report considers the consequences of the collapse of the unified decisionmaking system that had controlled the old Soviet military institution. It seeks to provide a benchmark for what has been lost with the disappearance of that central political-military mechanism and thus to help illuminate the choices facing the new, post-Soviet institution-builders.

The study was prepared under the sponsorship of the U.S. Army as part of a broad project initiated by the Policy and Strategy Program of RAND's Arroyo Center to examine the effect of Gorbachev's innovations on the struggle of conflicting interests within the Soviet elite.

This report should be of interest to members of the U.S. intelligence and policy communities and others concerned with the events in progress in the former Soviet Union. The analysis considers information available through March 1992.

THE ARROYO CENTER

The Arroyo Center is the U.S. Army's federally funded research and development center (FFRDC) for studies and analysis operated by RAND. The Arroyo Center provides the Army with objective, independent analytic research on major policy and organizational concerns, emphasizing mid- to long-term problems. Its research is carried out in four programs: Strategy and Doctrine, Force Development and Technology, Military Logistics, and Manpower and Training.

Army Regulation 5-21 contains basic policy for the conduct of the Arroyo Center. The Army provides continuing guidance and oversight through the Arroyo Center Policy Committee, which is cochaired by the Vice Chief of Staff and by the Assistant Secretary for Research, Development, and Acquisition. Arroyo Center work is performed under contract MDA 903-91-C-0006.

The Arroyo Center is housed in RAND's Army Research Division. RAND is a private, nonprofit institution that conducts analytic research on a wide range of public policy matters affecting the nation's security and welfare.

Lynn E. Davis is Vice President for the Army Research Division and Director of the Arroyo Center. Those interested in further information concerning the Arroyo Center should contact her office directly:

Lynn E. Davis
RAND
1700 Main Street
P.O. Box 2138
Santa Monica, CA 90407-2138

SUMMARY

The demise of the Soviet state has dramatically focused attention on the consequences of the collapse of the unified decisionmaking system that controlled the old Soviet military institution. This report seeks to provide a benchmark for what has been lost with the disappearance of that central political-military mechanism, and thus to help illuminate the choices facing the new, post-Soviet institution-builders.

THE GORBACHEV DEFENSE COUNCIL AND ITS PRECURSORS

At the time of Gorbachev's accession as party General Secretary in March 1985, the most important Soviet decisionmaking organ for national security was the Defense Council. This body and its various predecessors since Lenin's day had many differences but shared one central attribute: they served as the central locus of interaction between the political and military leaderships for the resolution of defense-related issues.

Invariably chaired by the Communist Party leader ever since Stalin's time, the Gorbachev Defense Council and its predecessors all sensitively reflected the leader's shifting relationships with his political colleagues as well as with the military elite. For that reason, the way this decisionmaking organ was run, the frequency with which it met, the men and institutions allowed to participate, and the matters considered all changed over time under Khrushchev, under Brezhnev, and under Gorbachev as well.

GORBACHEV'S INITIAL CHANGES

Soon after Gorbachev came to power in 1985, he, like those who came before him, set about modifying the Defense Council's structure and membership to suit his personal needs and his political agenda. One of his first steps was to broaden institutional representation on both the military and civilian sides. The Defense Council for the time being became considerably larger than it had been since Khrushchev's time, as Gorbachev brought all the important national security interests and players together around one table while at the same time significantly widening the definition of "national security" to include the foreign minister as well as an expanded group of key military figures. Gorbachev managed to exclude those party leaders, however important politically, whose jobs did not involve any national security matters.

Particularly important to the Soviet military was the fact that Gorbachev admitted to the inner sanctum one man—Foreign Minister Eduard Shevardnadze—who during the five years that he remained there was to prove hostile to the military leadership's view of Soviet security needs. On the other hand, the military retained traditional major structural advantages in the workings of the Gorbachev Defense Council, including the fact that the General Staff served as the Council's secretariat. The special leverage the military enjoyed because of this role became a sensitive point for the General Staff's relationship with the Politburo.

THE FOUR BROAD DEFENSE COUNCIL FUNCTIONS

What did Gorbachev's Defense Council do? Traditionally the most basic function was the decisionmaking role for resource allocation for **development and procurement of major weapons systems**.

Second, the Defense Council evaluated the possible consequences for the balance of forces of any unilateral Soviet steps to reduce weaponry. The Council, "with the participation of competent experts," is said to have **"elaborated"** all the Soviet Union's **"main military-political initiatives"** of this kind. These included such unilateral decisions as the announcement or revocation of moratoria on nuclear tests, all unilateral force reduction measures and force deployment changes, and the outlines of big new Soviet packages for mutual arms reduction.

Third, the Defense Council oversaw the **internal organization and deployment of the armed forces**, including *inter alia* such matters as "mobilization readiness plans" and draft and manpower policies. Hence, the Defense Council was responsible for reviewing and approving new plans for reorganization of the defense establishment as they were worked out by the General Staff.

And finally, the Defense Council approved changes in Soviet military **strategy and doctrine**. In 1989, during the Supreme Soviet debate over the confirmation of Defense Minister Yazov, Gorbachev went out of his way to emphasize that the Defense Council as a whole, and not Yazov or any other general, was the sole arbiter of Soviet military strategy.

THE ARMS CONTROL COORDINATING COMMISSION

Although it was the Defense Council that "elaborated" and "evaluated" Soviet unilateral Soviet military inititiatives, there was another powerful institution in the Gorbachev era that coordinated the evolving Soviet negotiating position in arms control talks. Within a year after Gorbachev took office, a special commission was set up by the Politburo to deal with "the military and technical aspects of international politics, including preparations for talks on arms reductions." This body built on precedents from earlier periods and was initially called, according to one insider, the "Political Commission." After the emergence of the executive presidency in 1990, this commission for arms control, like the Defense Council, was shifted to become subordinate to Gorbachev in his capacity as president. It was then reportedly renamed the "Group on Negotiations."

When this seven-man "Political Commission" of the Politburo was set up in 1986, Lev Zaykov was made its chairman, but his fellow Politburo members Shevardnadze and Aleksandr Yakovlev—the two foreign policy radicals—were also placed on the commission by Gorbachev. The other four commission members were the Defense Minister, the chief of the General Staff, the chairman of the KGB, and the most senior military-industrial leader.

THE COMMISSION'S "WORKING GROUP"

The Politburo commission was served by an interdepartmental working group. Chaired by First Deputy Chief of the General Staff Colonel General Bronislav Omelichev, this group also had seven members and apparently operated at the deputy minister level. The working group in turn was supported by a variety of departments, scientists, and experts in the military-industrial complex, notably including the defense department of the party Central Committee. The future coup conspirator Oleg Baklanov, who as Central Committee secretary supervised the military-industrial work of that party defense department from 1988 on, stated in the summer of 1990 that he was "involved in preparing the negotiating process," and Baklanov himself served as a member of the commission's working group.

Like the Defense Council, Gorbachev's new system for arms control policy coordination reflected an effort to broaden the base of institutional representation and also to provide at least somewhat greater political firepower to views differing from those of the military. As in the case of the Defense Council, the military leadership and its defense industry sympathizers from the start retained an extremely powerful position in the "working group" of the arms control commission. Nevertheless, the new arrangement, at least until 1990, did represent an evolution of Soviet decisionmaking practice in a direction unwelcome to the military, in two respects.

First, at the working level, the proliferation of institutions and individuals authorized to participate in the inner discussion of the pros and cons of ongoing negotiations probably served as an opening wedge, legitimating to some degree the much wider public discussion of military issues that Gorbachev, Yakovlev, and Shevardnadze began to encourage from 1987 on, to the chagrin of the military leadership.

And second, the makeup of the decisionmaking Politburo commission itself was surely unwelcome to the General Staff. The inclusion of Yakovlev as well as Shevardnadze—during the five years that they remained in place—substantially increased the political weight of the forces likely to endorse concessions to the West in the commission's discussions of several ongoing arms control negotiations.

THE NEW PRESIDENTIAL APPARAT AND BAKLANOV

This equation changed significantly during the last year of the USSR's existence, after Gorbachev in late 1990 temporarily moved to the right, Shevardnadze and Yakovlev departed, and Baklanov's role became magnified. The military position in the national security decisionmaking institutions then became much more predominant, and remained so until the August 1991 coup.

During this final year, a significant apparat concerned with defense and security affairs began to emerge in the office of President Gorbachev. From the fall of 1990 on, Oleg Baklanov directed a new department in Gorbachev's presidential staff for military questions, composed largely of former members of the defense department of the Central Committee. In April 1991, Gorbachev also appointed Baklanov First Deputy Chairman of the Defense Council. Gorbachev by this time had allowed an impressive combination of key national security decisionmaking functions to become concentrated in Baklanov's hands. Baklanov was exceptionally pugnacious in defending the military point of view. So long as he remained in place as the key figure of national security decisionmaking, the conservative perspective of the military-industrial establishment could be reinforced at all the key points—in the Defense Council, the General Staff, the Military-Industrial Commission, and the "military department" of the presidency.

THE CONSEQUENCES OF THE CENTRIFUGAL PROCESS

As it turned out, however, in 1991 the ongoing centrifugal process outside Moscow was to prove much more important for the future of the Defense Council—and for the Soviet military institution as a whole—than were all Gorbachev's reorganizations and appointments in the capital. During the winter of 1990, while military influence over the regime increased in Moscow, the military's ability to carry out its wishes went on decreasing everywhere outside Moscow. During the months leading up to the August coup, the leaders of the military-industrial complex discovered that the centrifugal process in the USSR steadily whittled away at their traditional ability to use central institutions to carry out unilateral decisions affecting the republics.

A leading example of this trend was the continued inability of the Defense Ministry and the Defense Council to compel the republics to fulfill conscription quotas. The steady fall in the rate of compliance with the semiannual call-up created a growing reality that was completely outside the decisionmaking framework: that is, the unplanned shrinking of the armed forces as a result of the center's steadily diminishing ability to enforce the draft.

Equally important, as the power of the purse gravitated away from the center in 1991, the military hardware program decisions and the overall military spending levels traditionally worked out and approved by the Defense Council now became increasingly vulnerable to pressure from the republics. The privileged position of military industry was already being weakened by the center's loss of control over the declining economy, and the centrifugal process immensely aggravated this trend. As 1991 went on, the republic leaders began to use the financial leverage they had seized—the new power to withhold money from the center—to press for radical further reductions in the central military budget.

Meanwhile, as the struggle over the new union treaty evolved, the leaders of Russia and Ukraine began to take organizational measures to try to force the center to confirm in the treaty an explicit transfer to the republics of authority over defense industrial plants on their territory. Simultaneously, the republics in the summer of 1991 pressed insistently for a fundamental reorganization of the existing defense decisionmaking structure, including admission of their representatives to the USSR Defense Council with an "absolute veto" over all decisions.

All this was anathema to the leaders of the central military-industrial complex who controlled the Defense Council. Thus both what had already happened and what was about to happen contributed to their decision to launch the August 1991 coup. A prominent motive was the hope to halt the centrifugal process by preventing the imminent signing of a union treaty that would formalize a vast further reduction in the degree of influence over the national security decisionmaking process they still enjoyed.

THE INSTITUTIONAL CONSEQUENCES OF THE FAILED COUP

After the collapse of the coup, Gorbachev's decisionmaking arrangements for national security were discredited, particularly since so many of the leading figures of the old institutions were now in prison. In the fall of 1991, repeated efforts were made to create new interrepublic defense coordination mechanisms that would reconcile the incompatible demands of centralized control and real republic sovereignty. However, this effort was stymied because certain republics—particularly Ukraine—showed increasing hostility toward preserving any form of central, all-union authority. Subsequently, Russian President Yeltsin's decision to cease funding most of the central governmental apparat inevitably also accelerated a tendency toward formal division of the Soviet armed forces. Although Yeltsin for the time being continued Russian funding for the Soviet Ministry of Defense, and thus maintained the pretense that this was an ongoing all-union institution independent of Russia, few could believe that contention once this ministry was left standing alone without a surrounding all-union government.

The Ukrainian leaders had in any case already made it clear that they had no doubt that Russia would control the Moscow machinery of the Soviet army and that they were unwilling to remain subject to that machinery. By mid-October, the Ukrainian leaders had announced that they intended to create their own sizable army from the Soviet general-purpose forces stationed in Ukraine. Equally important, they made it clear that no general-purpose ground forces not subordinated to Kiev would be allowed to remain in Ukraine. A strong Ukrainian consensus soon emerged on this point, and was eventually reinforced by the results of the Ukrainian referendum on independence.

Soviet nuclear forces meanwhile presented a problem of a different kind, particularly because here outside pressures were directly involved. The ongoing disintegration of the Soviet Union evoked alarm in the West over the dangerous possibilities inherent in any weakening of central controls over nuclear weapons. The concern was particularly great with respect to the thousands of tactical nuclear weapons scattered throughout the Soviet Union, which Gorbachev had now agreed to destroy.

THE COMMONWEALTH AND THE DECISIONMAKING SYSTEM

Once Ukraine in early December 1991 approved a referendum approving independence, both the old union and and its military control structure were effectively doomed. Therefore, a week later Yeltsin finally moved to reach agreement with Ukraine and Belarus to put an end to the USSR and to create a "Commonwealth of Independent States" (CIS). The Minsk declaration that initially embodied the commonwealth agreement pledged to "preserve and support common military and strategic space under a common command." But there was no consensus on the meaning of this vague formula, as soon became clear.

On the nuclear side of the issue, a measure of understanding seemed to be reached under Western prodding. In a Strategic Forces Agreement signed by the CIS members, Ukraine agreed to dismantle nuclear weapons on its territory and to allow such weapons pending their removal to remain under the control of a new Combined Strategic Forces Command. The new agreement specified that this command would control not only strategic weapons systems, but also the air force, navy, and air defense commands, the space command, the airborne troops, and military intelligence. These provisions about the strategic portions of the armed forces were, however, ambiguous and soon became a matter of dispute. Even Ukrainian consent to transfer tactical nuclear weapons from Ukraine to Russia for dismantling was to be temporarily placed in doubt in March 1992, when Ukrainian President Kravchuk, intent on using the issue for bargaining purposes, announced a halt to such transfers. Eventually, however, Kravchuk relented under Western pressure, and the movement of these weapons to Russia was resumed and completed.

Meanwhile, a parallel attempt was made to transform the bulk of the army—the nonstrategic Soviet general-purpose troops—into joint CIS forces. But this effort was crippled when Ukraine and a few other republics refused to participate. By January, as Ukraine pressed the issue of the allegiance of the hundreds of thousands of general-purpose ground troops on its soil, it had won over the bulk of the local command structure. Simultaneously, the ambiguities in the December understanding about the Combined Strategic Forces Command also came to the surface, since a protracted dispute now emerged between Ukraine and Russia over the definition of "strategic forces," a term the General Staff had always used very broadly. Mutual animosity soon developed over the issue of which units of the Black Sea Fleet would fall into this "strategic" category—and remain with the CIS—and which should be considered general-purpose ships and be taken over by Ukraine.

Thus, by early 1992, huge gaps had suddenly appeared in the traditional all-union military structure. The remaining parts of that structure were now functioning in the name of the Commonwealth but were more and more clearly identified with Russia. In Russia itself, however, the building of such new institutions was at first delayed by the felt need to maintain the Commonwealth facade, to bridge the gap until more permanent understandings could be reached between Russia and other republics regarding the status of the forces and weaponry of the former Soviet Union deployed outside Russia. The Russian military leaders feared that if Russia took formal control of the forces nominally subordinated to the Commonwealth, there would be an accelerated tendency of republics to take the Ukrainian path, to create armies of their own, and to advance unilateral claims to the weapons and soldiers stationed on their soil.

On the other hand, many democrats in Moscow were alarmed at what they regarded as the dangerous lack of subordination of the heirs of the old Soviet military establishment to the Russian state and to popular control. At the same time, many in the army shared great unease over the army's lack of formal subordination to a state, the lack of a clear mission and doctrine, and the absence of a formal structure linking it to the political leadership. The dilemma was compounded by the widespread reluctance of other republics to allow the CIS to build its own political-military superstructure because of fears that it would revive the apparatus of a new central state.

In March, Yeltsin took a small step toward resolving the dilemma when he at last announced the creation of a Russian Ministry of Defense, headed, temporarily, by himself. Initially, the ministry was not yet given any functions, and Yeltsin sidestepped the issue of a Russian army by assuming control of the forces actually controlled by the CIS and simultaneously redesignating them back to CIS control. By so doing, however, Russia had edged closer to the Rubicon: the negotiation of bilateral or multilateral mutual security or status-of-forces agreements between Russia and other republics that would define the terms under which Russian troops would in future years remain deployed outside Russia. When and if these understandings are finally reached, Russia's need for a Commonwealth title for its general-purpose forces may recede, although the requirement for a CIS umbrella for strategic forces may endure much longer.

In the meantime, the emergence of the Russian Ministry of Defense has brought to the surface a heated political struggle in Moscow over the future structure and orientation of the Russian military establishment and the organizations that will control it. One of the issues will inevitably be the ideological leanings of the actors involved in whatever new supreme institutions for national security coordinating and decisionmaking eventually reemerge in Russia. A step was taken toward resolution of this issue when legislation was enacted creating a Russian Federation Security Council, designed to make policy on issues of domestic as well as foreign security. Even after Yeltsin named a professional soldier—Army General Pavel Grachev—to succeed himself as Minister of Defense, rather than the civilian minister sought by many Russian democrats, the democrats could hope that a barrier had been created to the resurrection of General Staff control of the Council, since the General Staff could not appropriately serve as the secretariat for the Council's extensive nonmilitary work.

Nevertheless, the key question of the nature of the supporting apparatus for the Defense Council remained to be determined, and here, unfortunately, Russia still has before it the ill-fated model of the network that supported the defense councils of the past in the Central Committee departments and the presidential office. In the spring of 1992, many reactionary veterans of Baklanov's now defunct military-political support machinery were waiting to be called back to action if Yeltsin resuscitated that machinery. The possibility that such individuals could return—and could eventually seek to revive the attitudes of the past—is underlined by the continued survival of reactionary veterans of the Soviet past in other Russian organizations, notably the successor organization to the KGB. The direction taken in future years by a new Russian national security decisionmaking organ may therefore be heavily influenced by the personnel choices made by Yeltsin at the outset. The long-term importance of this issue was further underscored in the spring of 1992 by disturbing signs that Yeltsin was coming under increasing pressure to make concessions to the traditionally dominant forces in the military institution.

ACKNOWLEDGMENTS

The author would like to thank Benjamin Lambeth and Edward Warner for their helpful comments on an early draft of this report. He also wishes to express appreciation to the International Institute for Strategic Studies in London and to the Radio Free Europe/Radio Liberty Research Institute in Munich, where research for parts of the study was performed.

CONTENTS

PREFACE iii
SUMMARY... v
ACKNOWLEDGMENTS xv

Section
1. INTRODUCTION 1
2. THE PRECURSORS OF THE GORBACHEV
   DEFENSE COUNCIL............................ 2
   Khrushchev's Supreme Military Council 3
   Brezhnev's Two Versions of the Defense Council....... 5
   The Public Surfacing of the Defense Council.......... 8
   The Defense Council During the Interregnum 10
3. THE DEFENSE COUNCIL UNDER GORBACHEV 12
   The Four Broad Defense Council Functions 16
   The Main Military Council 19
4. THE COMMISSION FOR ARMS CONTROL
   COORDINATION............................... 22
   The Commission's "Working Group" 23
   The Two Adverse Effects for the Military 25
5. POLICY STRUGGLE IN THE TWO
   DECISIONMAKING ORGANS..................... 27
   Early Contention over Personnel Changes 27
   The Krasnoyarsk Radar 29
   The Struggle over INF 30
   The Struggle over Conventional Force Reduction 31
   Shevardnadze's Attack on Past Defense Council
      Decisions 32
   The Council Debate and the Shift Toward
      Reductions 34
   The Breakdown of the Coordination Machinery over
      CFE 37
6. THE LAST PHASE OF THE SOVIET STATE AND
   THE DECLINE OF CENTRAL SECURITY
   DECISIONMAKING 41
   The March 1990 Struggle over the Defense Council 41

	The Council Revives as Gorbachev Moves to the Right	45
	The Security Council	49
	The New Presidential Apparat, Boldin, and Baklanov	50
	The Momentous Consequences of the Centrifugal Process	54
	The Pressures and Inducements to Attempt a Coup	59
7.	THE END OF THE SOVIET STATE AND THE FUTURE OF DEFENSE DECISIONMAKING	61
	The First Institutional Results of the Failed Coup	61
	The Last Appearance of the USSR Defense Council	63
	The Impact of Fragmentation on Defense Decisionmaking	64
	The Nuclear Problem	67
	The Commonwealth	69
	The Impasse over Joint Armed Forces	71
	The Future of Defense Decisionmaking Institutions	72

1. INTRODUCTION

The demise of the Soviet state has dramatically focused attention on the consequences of the collapse of the unified decisionmaking system that controlled the old Soviet military institution. This report seeks to provide a benchmark for what has been lost with the disappearance of that central political-military mechanism, and thus to help illuminate the choices facing the new, post-Soviet institution-builders.

To this end, the report uses fragmentary past evidence and many revelations of recent years to sketch the evolution of the Soviet national security decisionmaking system from its earliest days through the dramatic changes of the Gorbachev era. The bulk of the discussion concerns two key central institutions of the old Soviet regime: the Defense Council and the leadership's commission for coordination of arms control decisions. The study traces the factors that progressively undermined these institutions in the last years of the Soviet regime. It explains how the despair of those in the military-industrial complex who had traditionally dominated this system prior to its collapse helped trigger the August 1991 abortive attempt at a coup, whose failure in turn precipitated the final downfall of the Soviet state. The report concludes by examining the issues confronted by the new Commonwealth of Independent States and the individual republics in dealing with the heritage of the old decisionmaking system.

2. THE PRECURSORS OF THE GORBACHEV DEFENSE COUNCIL

At the time of Gorbachev's accession as Communist Party General Secretary in March 1985, the most important Soviet decisionmaking organ for national security was the Defense Council. This body had had a series of antecedents throughout Soviet history with significantly varying purposes and composition, ranging from the Labor and Defense Council of Lenin's day,[1] to the State Defense Committee set up by Stalin to run the Soviet war effort during World War II, to the Supreme Military Council described by the British intelligence agent Penkovskiy in Khrushchev's day, to the Defense Council that emerged in Brezhnev's time as the immediate predecessor of Gorbachev's rather different organization of the same name.

Although these various bodies had major differences in function, makeup, and method of operation, they had some features in common. The most important common denominator was that they all served as the central locus of interaction between the political and military leaderships for the resolution of defense-related issues. More specifically, apart from whatever else they did, the Defense Council and its predecessors were concerned with broad decisions about hardware development and procurement, with decisions governing military organization and deployment, and with military strategy.

However, the Gorbachev Defense Council and its forerunners were also political bodies gradually adjusting to the changing political realities of the time, rather than permanent, inflexible bureaucratic edifices.[2] Consequently, the way the Defense Council and its predecessors were run, the frequency with which they met, the men and institutions allowed to participate, and the matters considered all

---

[1] Lenin's Labor and Defense Council was established in April 1920 under the Council of People's Commissars to "guide the work of all departments in the sphere of defense and economic development," and "played a major role in bulding up the Red Army and Navy." The Labor and Defense Council was itself a reorganized version of a "Council of Workers' and Peasants' Defense," which Lenin had originally set up under his chairmanship in November 1918 to "mobilize the republic's human and material resources" during the period of foreign military intervention and civil war. (V. N. Kudryavtsev, A. I. Lukyanov, and G. Kh. Shakhnazarov, *The Soviet Constitution: A Dictionary*, Progress Publishers, Moscow, 1986, pp. 81–82.)

[2] As one knowledgeable source put it, the Defense Council was, "after all, more a political organ than, as many suppose, a purely military one." (Col. Gen. Boris Gromov, interviewed in *Dialog* (Moscow), No. 18, December 1990.)

altered over time. As the discussion below will show, the Defense Council and its predecessors displayed the same accordion-like periodic expansion and contraction characteristic of the Soviet state administrative structure as a whole.

Although important lines of continuity obviously existed between the Gorbachev Defense Council and its forerunners, Western generalizations about which Soviet officials did or did not belong to these bodies *ex officio* were therefore misleading when applied over long stretches of time, and certainly to periods of more than a decade or so. Fluctuations in the organization of the Soviet national security decisionmaking bodies never ceased, and dramatically increased in the final, crisis year of the Soviet state.

A decisive factor in shaping and reshaping the Soviet decisionmaking process was the political status of the man at the top. Invariably and inevitably chaired by the Communist Party leader since Stalin's time (because control over the defense sphere was an essential aspect of the party leader's power), the Defense Council and its predecessors always sensitively reflected the leader's shifting relationship with his political colleagues as well as with the military elite. Thus, it is hardly surprising that until the Labor and Defense Council inherited from Lenin was abolished by Stalin in 1937, its decisions "in the last analysis were taken by Stalin";[3] nor that during the war Stalin's State Defense Committee[4] had an even simpler arrangement, since "there were no meetings of the SDC in the usual meaning of the word—i.e., meetings with a definite agenda, secretaries and minutes."[5] Instead, the key Politburo members and military leaders who were appointed to this committee met with Stalin as necessary, singly or in groups, to obtain approval of proposed decisions.

KHRUSHCHEV'S SUPREME MILITARY COUNCIL

By Khrushchev's time, in the early 1960s, the situation was rather different. A Supreme Military Council attached to the party leader-

---

[3]Marshal Zhukov statement in *Voyennyy Vestnik*, No. 20 (26), October 1987.

[4]This committee was set up immediately after the Nazi attack, four years after the abolition of its predecessor.

[5]*Pravda*, June 30, 1986. The wartime State Defense Committee of course had far broader functions than the postwar Defense Council was to have under Stalin's successors. The State Defense Committee supervised, among other things, the mobilization of the entire economy to defend the country. In the post-Stalin era, there was often considerable Soviet controversy about the adequacy of mobilization plans to convert the peacetime Defense Council into a new version of the State Defense Committee in the event of a sudden wartime emergency.

ship had come into being and held formal meetings. After dissolving the State Defense Committee at the close of the war in 1945, Stalin in 1949 established a Supreme Military Council under his chairmanship to facilitate decisionmaking for the Cold War, and it is this organization that Khrushchev apparently inherited and developed in the form Penkovskiy described.

We have from Penkovskiy a valuable if somewhat fuzzy snapshot of the military decisionmaking process in the early 1960s, obtained from a council participant.[6] Meetings of the Supreme Military Council at this point were always attended by "a few" members of the party leadership. They were chaired by Khrushchev, and his three most senior political colleagues—Central Committee secretaries Frol Kozlov and Mikhail Suslov and First Deputy Premier Anastas Mikoyan—were also council members. In Khrushchev's absence, the council was chaired by Kozlov or Mikoyan. The Minister of Defense and the commanders-in-chief of the service arms were "automatically" members, but some service chiefs might not attend if subjects not concerning them were under discussion. The council generally met at regular intervals, but might be convened more frequently if required by "extraordinary events." Decisions regarding defense production and defense expenditures were prominent in the council's activity, and Penkovskiy asserts that party Presidium [Politburo] member Leonid Brezhnev was heavily involved in these military-industrial matters, implying that he also participated in at least some council deliberations.

Kozlov and Suslov were deeply interested in defense questions and seem to have been generally sympathetic to military needs, but were unwilling to make controversial decisions on defense expenditures at council meetings held in Khrushchev's absence.[7] For his part, Khrushchev sought to use the Supreme Military Council as his personal vehicle, sometimes employing it "as a substitute for the Minister of Defense, making decisions concerning the least important

---

[6]Oleg Penkovskiy, *The Penkovskiy Papers*, Doubleday, Garden City, New York, 1965, pp. 233–234. Penkovskiy obtained his information from Chief Marshal of Aviation Sergey Varentsov, a close friend who was a member of the Supreme Military Council. Penkovskiy's information is credible in the sense that it is probably not willfully invented or distorted, but it nevertheless reflects only his fragmentary recollections of Varentsov's statements at different times. In particular, the depiction of the membership of the Supreme Military Council obtained from Varentsov may well be incomplete. Moreover, Varentsov's description of the behavior of participants certainly reflected his personal prejudices.

[7]*Ibid.*, pp. 209, 300–301. Varentsov, impatient at this behavior, is said to have longed for the days of Stalin, when there was no problem in obtaining authoritative decisions.

matters," and often using it to bypass the minister, issuing orders directly to service commanders.[8] Defense Minister Malinovskiy, meanwhile, is said by Penkovskiy's eyewitness to have consistently behaved at council meetings as Khrushchev's toady, keeping silent until Khrushchev had spoken, and then invariably expressing agreement.[9]

This post-Stalin decisionmaking system and set of relationships had a specific political backdrop: it existed in the aftermath of Khrushchev's 1957 purge of the previous Defense Minister, Marshal Zhukov, who was later accused, among other things, of having sought to usurp control over the Supreme Military Council "despite the fact that it included members of the Party Presidium as well as military and political leaders of the army and navy."[10] The subservient behavior in the council attributed to Zhukov's successor Malinovskiy was thus a consequence of Zhukov's fate, and Khrushchev's humiliation of the marshals was also manifested in many other ways. This treatment by Khrushchev bred a deep resentment in the military leadership that was still reverberating in Gorbachev's day, and that conditioned the reactions of some military leaders to the unwelcome changes Gorbachev introduced.

BREZHNEV'S TWO VERSIONS OF THE DEFENSE COUNCIL

The anger of the generals at their treatment by the party leadership under Khrushchev produced a campaign for institutional changes after his fall in October 1964. Between 1965 and early 1967, some elements of the Soviet military leadership pressed for a modification of party-military joint organizational arrangements at the highest level to enlarge the military voice and to reduce the likelihood of repeating what Chief of the General Staff M. V. Zakharov called the "very expensive" and "irreparable" damage done by Khrushchev's management of military affairs.[11] In January 1966, one general called for the creation of a "single military-political organ" that would "unite" the political and military leadership both in wartime and "in times of peace," and that would give due weight to professional military exper-

---

[8]*Ibid.*, p. 240.

[9]*Ibid.*, p. 310. For this reason, among others, Malinovskiy was said to be not respected in the General Staff. All these statements, of course, reflect Varentsov's personal biases.

[10]Yu. P. Petrov, *Partinoye stroitelstvo v sovetskoy armii i flote, 1918-1961*, Moscow, 1964, pp. 305–306, cited in Thomas Wolfe, *The Soviet Military Scene: Institutional and Defense Policy Considerations*, RAND, RM-4913-PR, 1966, pp. 11–12.

[11]*Krasnaya Zvezda*, February 4, 1965.

tise.¹² A year later, another stated that in the event of war supreme authority would be vested in special "military-political organs" which "are already now being created."¹³ In March 1967, on the very day that Defense Minister Malinovskiy died, another senior officer again publicly stressed the need for a "collective organ" of national defense leadership premised on the "unity" of political and military leaders.¹⁴

The goals of this military agitation appeared to be a revision of the defense decisionmaking process to give greater weight to professional military opinion than Khrushchev had allowed, and also to make possible a smoother conversion of that process to wartime status in the event of war. It is not clear how far Brezhnev's organizational changes represented concessions to this viewpoint, since the available public information about Brezhnev's Defense Council is even more fragmentary than the data about Khrushchev's Supreme Military Council. What does seem reasonably apparent, and significant for the future evolution of the council, is the following:

First, the change in name from Supreme Military Council to Defense Council probably occurred long before the Soviets began to publicize the new name in 1976. The name change was probably associated with changes in the council membership put into effect not long after the Brezhnev cabal seized power from Khrushchev in 1964. The participation of Politburo members in the national security decisionmaking organ now became somewhat more restricted, and remained so for the next eight years. Indirect but persuasive evidence suggests that during this period the two ranking Central Committee secretaries after Brezhnev—Suslov and Andrey Kirilenko—no longer participated in the council, as Suslov and Kozlov had done under Khrushchev. The only full Politburo members who did regularly participate until 1973 were General Secretary Brezhnev, Premier Kosygin, and President Podgornyy.¹⁵ Certain other officials with relevant functions

---

¹²Col. Gen. N. Lomov in the January 1966 issue of the restricted Ministry of Defense publication *Voyennaya mysl'* (Military Thought), subsequently made publicly available in the West.

¹³Maj. Gen. V. Zemskov in *Krasnaya Zvezda*, January 5, 1967.

¹⁴Lt. Gen. I. Zavyalov in *Krasnaya Zvezda*, March 31, 1967. Grechko succeeded Malinovskiy the following month.

¹⁵See Tommy L. Whitton, "The Defense Council and Military Obituaries: A Working Hypothesis," *Air Force Strategic Studies Newsletter*, April 25, 1983, which is the best-informed unclassified statement on the matter. Although citing only evidence from Politburo signatures of military obituaries, Whitton's judgment is supported by a Soviet account of a formal reception of the entire military leadership that occurred in early April 1967, during the brief interval between Malinovskiy's death and Grechko's appointment to replace him. The Soviet press reported that Brezhnev, Podgornyy, and Kosygin received a large group of the leading commanders, who heard Brezhnev talk

who were not then full Politburo members—such as the Central Committee secretary in charge of defense industry (Dmitriy Ustinov), the defense minister, and the chief of the General Staff—apparently also belonged to the Defense Council and regularly interacted there with the three full Politburo members. They were joined on an *ad hoc* basis, but only as occasion required, by others such as the military service chiefs, the chairman of the Military-Industrial Commission (VPK), and the chairman of the KGB.

This system seems to have reflected a conscious and formalized effort to bring together the key institutional representatives in the overlapping realms of Soviet defense, while removing (for the time being) those who did not have direct responsibilities in defense matters. This change was consistent with the new Brezhnev regime's increased stress on order, organizational symmetry, "scientific" process, and formality, in contrast with Khrushchev's arbitrary and haphazard way of doing things. It may also have represented a gesture toward the military demands cited above for a revision of the way Khrushchev had organized the Supreme Military Council.

At the same time, by including certain senior Politburo members while (for a time) excluding others whose political status would have entitled them to seats in Khrushchev's version of the Defense Council, Brezhnev apparently sought to enhance his personal political leverage in the infighting that went on within the party leadership. Thus, for example, in June 1967, at a confrontation at a party Central Committee plenum after the Arab-Israeli Six-Day War, Brezhnev apparently relied on the special information available to him as Defense Council chairman to rebut charges of Soviet military unpreparedness during the war that had been made during the plenum by Moscow party first secretary Nikolay Yegorychev, evidently at the instigation of Brezhnev's Politburo opponent Aleksandr Shelepin, who was not a member of the Defense Council.[16]

The second point to be made about the Defense Council under Brezhnev is that the arrangements made after Khrushchev's fall evidently did not last. There is reason to believe that beginning in 1973, the Politburo membership in the Defense Council was again revised, and the two ranking Central Committee secretaries after Brezhnev—Suslov and Kirilenko—were readmitted, while the earlier triumvirate

---

about "certain questions of military development." No other Politburo members were reported present.

[16]See Harry Gelman, *The Brezhnev Politburo and the Decline of Detente*, Cornell University Press, Ithaca, 1984, pp. 96–98.

of General Secretary Brezhnev, Premier Kosygin, and President Podgornyy remained, along with the sixth key civilian, Central Committee secretary for military industry (and alternate Politburo member) Dmitriy Ustinov.[17]

This change is likely to have reflected the altered political situation in the elite in a period of extended strategic arms negotiations with the United States. It gave a larger segment of the Politburo[18] continual access to military data and briefings relevant to those negotiations, while enabling the Politburo to bring considerably greater political weight to bear in its Defense Council dealings with the marshals. This consideration no doubt became particularly important after the Defense Minister, Marshal Grechko, became a full Politburo member in 1973. In 1979, the new pattern was reconfirmed, when a Central Committee official stated privately that even in the Defense Council, although the professional military were represented in greater strength than in the Politburo, "they are not in the majority."[19] At the same time, this trend in the second half of the Brezhnev period toward wider Politburo participation in the Defense Council also seems to have reflected the increasing tension in the Politburo itself as the economic costs of the growth of Soviet military spending mounted.

THE PUBLIC SURFACING OF THE DEFENSE COUNCIL

Less than three years after revision of its membership, the existence of the Defense Council was at last publicly acknowledged (in obscure fashion) by the Soviet Union,[20] and a year later this body was, in effect, legitimized. In 1977, the new Soviet constitution sponsored by

---

[17]See the discussion in Whitton, *op. cit.* Whitton cites evidence to suggest that when Chernenko took Kirilenko's place in the Central Committee secretariat in 1981, he took his seat on the Defense Council as well. Similarly, Whitton's evidence strongly implies that after Suslov died in 1982 and was replaced in the party secretariat by Yuriy Andropov, Andropov obtained the *ex officio* seat on the Defense Council that he had lacked as KGB chairman.

[18]Minus Podgornyy, who was subsequently dropped from the political leaderhip and the Defense Council when Brezhnev usurped his job as Chairman of the Supreme Soviet—titular president—in 1977.

[19]Valentin Falin, quoted in the *Washington Star*, July 15, 1979, cited in Hakan Karlsson, "The Defense Council of the USSR," *Cooperation and Conflict*, No. 2, 1988, p. 75.

[20]The first bare mention of the Defense Council was made in the entry on Brezhnev (identifying him as its chairman) in *Sovetskaya voyennaya entsiklopediya*, Vol. 1, Voyenizdat, Moscow, 1976, p. 588, passed for printing on November 5, 1975. (Cited by Elizabeth Teague, "The Soviet Defense Council—Modern Successor to the Wartime GKO," Radio Liberty (RL) 246/8/81, June 19, 1981.)

Brezhnev announced laconically that "the Presidium of the USSR Supreme Soviet is responsible for forming the Defense Council of the USSR and approving its composition." The regime later claimed that this provision had been intended "to emphasize the importance of the body and the fact that this is a body of the Soviet state."[21] But there was to be no elaboration until well into the Gorbachev era.

The motivation for declassifying and formalizing the existence of the Defense Council (if little else about it) was, once again, twofold: on the one hand, it reflected the changing relationship among the Politburo oligarchs; and on the other, it reflected shifts in their dealings with the military leaders.

There can be little doubt that the main consideration for Brezhnev was the opportunity for self-aggrandizement vis-à-vis his colleagues. The unveiling of a constitutional rationale for the Defense Council was preceded and followed by public statements revealing and emphasizing to the political elite the fact that it was Brezhnev who chaired the council. Meanwhile, Brezhnev seized the occasion of the adoption of the new Constitution to further strengthen his position by replacing Podgornyy as Chairman of the Presidium of the Supreme Soviet, or titular president. In this post, he would among other things "form" the Defense Council, the body which he had already disclosed that he chaired as a result of his position as party General Secretary.[22] At the same time, Brezhnev benefited politically from the failure of the new constitution to list the other members of the Defense Council, or the positions that would qualify incumbents for council membership. Although this striking omission was consistent with traditional Soviet notions of secrecy, it also served Brezhnev's purposes in dealings with his colleagues because it implied that it was proper that he have discretion in the matter.

And finally, this formalization of Brezhnev's already existing power to shape and lead the Defense Council was doubtless also intended to assist him in dealing with the generals by magnifying his stature in his national security role. It is noteworthy that this change followed the death of Defense Minister Marshal Grechko the year before, the appointment of the civilian military-industrial specialist Dmitriy

---

[21] V. N. Kudryavtsev, A. I. Lukyanov, and G. Kh. Shakhnazarov, *op cit.* in footnote 1.

[22] Indeed, it is not unlikely that when he proposed to the Politburo that he replace Podgornyy as chairman of the Presidium of the Supreme Soviet, Brezhnev cited the new draft constitutional provision as one justification. The rationalization would be that now that the Supreme Soviet Presidium had been given explicit responsibility for "forming" the Defense Council, the council's chairman should also head the Presidium.

Ustinov to replace him, and the somewhat ludicrous designations of both Ustinov and Brezhnev as Marshals of the Soviet Union. Further along the same line, it was not coincidental that only a few months after the announcement of Brezhnev's new constitutional role, the Soviet press for the first time disclosed that he was "Supreme Commander in Chief of the Soviet Armed Forces."[23] Like many of Brezhnev's subsequent efforts to create for himself a fraudulent military glory, these measures reflected not only his wish to inflate his personal stature, but also the common interest of the Politburo in enhancing civilian authority within the Defense Council.

THE DEFENSE COUNCIL DURING THE INTERREGNUM

Although there is little available evidence about the makeup and functioning of the Defense Council in the interregnum period between the death of Brezhnev in October 1982 and the accession of Gorbachev in March 1985, certain observations about this period seem justified.

First, the party leader's role as chairman of the Defense Council continued to be a significant consideration in the political byplay among the party oligarchs. After Yuriy Andropov succeeded Brezhnev, and again after Konstantin Chernenko succeeded Andropov, gratuitous announcements were made to emphasize the fact that the new party leader also wore this second "hat."[24] It would appear that by the time of Brezhnev's death, the publicity he had given to the existence of the Defense Council had heightened the importance for each new General Secretary of confirming to the broad political elite that he had indeed inherited this vital attribute of his office.

Second, it was during this period of the interregnum that the role of the General Staff in running the machinery of the Defense Council seems for the first time to have become a political issue within the regime. That apparently happened as a consequence of the civil-military friction that had grown since Brezhnev's final years as a result of Soviet resource constraints. More particularly, Chief of the General Staff Nikolay Ogarkov's insubordinate reaction to those constraints brought to the fore the issue of the General Staff's relationship to the Defense Council. There is evidence to suggest that General Secretary Andropov some months before his death had begun to consider a radical reform that would have removed the General Staff from

---

[23]*Voyenny vestnik*, No. 10, October 1987.

[24]As will be seen, in early 1987 Gorbachev was to continue this tradition.

continuing to act as the working secretariat of the Defense Council. This issue will be considered later in greater detail during the discussion of the council's functions.

Finally, there is recent evidence to show that after Brezhnev's 1973 expansion of the Defense Council to include the two ranking Central Committee secretaries who were not otherwise concerned with defense matters, his successor Andropov again reversed this practice. Mikhail Gorbachev has stated that even he, the senior civilian Politburo and party secretariat member who was most closely allied with Andropov, was not allowed access to defense economic data.[25] Andropov, like Brezhnev during his first eight years, apparently sought to restrict access to defense information, even among key Politburo colleagues who did not have national security responsibilities, in order to enhance his own leverage within the leadership. It also seems likely that Andropov was particularly concerned to keep his Brezhnevite adversary Chernenko out of the Defense Council, and this would have been difficult if Gorbachev, who was nominally junior to Chernenko in both the Politburo and the secretariat, had been admitted.

To sum up thus far: throughout the thirty-two years from Stalin's death to Gorbachev's accession as General Secretary, the Defense Council and its predecessors continued to display the periodic expansion and contraction characteristic of all Soviet institutional structures.[26] The mix of participants kept changing back and forth, partly because of evolving views as to how the institution should function, but mostly because of changing political relationships on both the civilian and the military sides.

---

[25]"Even Yuriy Vladimorovich Andropov, to whom I was bound by 20 years of friendship, even he said then that we younger ones were poking around where we shouldn't be. That it was none of our business. [Central Committee secretaries] N. I. Ryzhkov, V. I. Dolgikh and I were not given access to the budget, to data on military spending. After all, at the time I was a member of the Politburo and was conducting meetings of the Central Committee's Secretariat. That was the situation." (Gorbachev speech of December 7, 1990, *Pravda*, December 10, 1990.)

[26]This repetitive expansion and contraction is reflected, for example, in the wall chart called *Evolution of the Central Administrative Structure of the USSR, 1917–1979*, National Foreign Assessment Center, CR 79-10123, Washington, D.C., August 1979. A somewhat similar phenomenon is visible in the long-term evolution of the party Politburo.

3. THE DEFENSE COUNCIL UNDER GORBACHEV

Soon after Gorbachev came to power in 1985, he, like those who came before him, set about modifying the Defense Council's structure and membership to suit his personal needs and his political agenda. The new Defense Council arrangements introduced by Gorbachev appear to have endured with only modest changes through his first five years. However, after he assumed the executive presidency in the spring of 1990, the Defense Council—for reasons discussed below—apparently entered a final period of great uncertainty and flux that went on until the final collapse of the Soviet system twenty-one months later.

When Gorbachev first took over the leadership, the Defense Council he inherited was, according to him, in a sorry state: "It used to work spasmodically and was merely formal." (This is credible, since we know from other testimony that the Politburo had also come to meet infrequently and irregularly in the late Brezhnev period.) This atrophy of the Defense Council's functions had "led to the concentration of the whole problem literally in the hands of several men . . . if not into just one man's hands, and we are reaping the fruit of this. . . ."[1] Consequently, "the Defense Council as a whole had to be decisively restructured," in order to "revive the Defense Council decisively and put it in the role, at the level, which it should be playing."

One of the first steps Gorbachev took in order to "decisively restructure" the Defense Council was to broaden institutional representation on both sides of the council table. The Defense Council for the time being became considerably larger than it had been since Khrushchev's time.

On the military side, in addition to the Defense Minister, council membership was now extended to "the main command personnel of the Armed Forces, but not all of them . . . precisely the main personnel, only a handful."[2] This formula is somewhat ambiguous, but it does seem likely that when he reorganized the Defense Council in 1985 Gorbachev invited not only the three First Deputy Ministers of Defense to participate, but also most if not all of the heads of the branches of service at the deputy defense minister level. Moreover,

---

[1] Gorbachev statement in Yazov confirmation debate, July 3, 1989.
[2] *Ibid.*

one particular officer who also became a council member at that time had a less immediate stake in the council's deliberations over weapons procurement than most of the deputy ministers—the chief of the Main Political Directorate of the armed forces, Army General Aleksey Lizichev.[3] Obviously, under these circumstances the most important Soviet soldier after the defense minister—Chief of the General Staff and First Deputy Minister of Defense Marshal Akhromeyev—was necessarily a participant, as he frequently confirmed.

By including the service chiefs (or most of them), Gorbachev was reverting to the practice followed by Khrushchev[4] and departing from Brezhnev's more restricted model. As noted previously, in the late Brezhnev period, according to knowledgeable Soviet testimony, the military representatives on the Defense Council were outnumbered by civilians,[5] and service chiefs were invited to attend only occasionally, on an individual, *ad hoc* basis.

At the same time, Gorbachev also altered and enlarged the Defense Council on the civilian side. As had been the practice under Brezhnev, the council continued to include the General Secretary (Gorbachev) as chairman, as well as the premier at the time (Nikolay Ryzhkov), and the man who was then the senior Central Committee secretary in charge of military industry (Lev Zaykov, later replaced by Oleg Baklanov). It would appear (although it is somewhat less certain) that the chairman of the Military-Industrial Commission (the VPK), who coordinated military industry under Zaykov's supervision, was also placed on Gorbachev's Defense Council as a full member.[6] But from the beginning Gorbachev went beyond this, and added the foreign minister[7] (his close ally at the time, Eduard Shevardnadze), as well as the KGB chairman[8] (in 1985, Viktor Chebrikov, and from

---

[3]Lizichev's statement in an address to Congress of People's Deputies, Moscow Television, June 6, 1989 (FBIS-USSR, June 7, 1989, p. 18). Lizichev had protocol equivalence to a First Deputy Minister of Defense, but he was less immediately affected than were the service chiefs by the hardware development and procurement issues so prominent in the Defense Council debates. Consequently, if he was admitted to the council, they certainly should have been.

[4]See Oleg Penkovskiy, *op. cit.*, pp. 233–234.

[5]See Falin statement cited in footnote 19, Section 2.

[6]Gorbachev speaks of "the comrades in charge of military industry" as belonging to the Defense Council. Whereas Zaykov definitely was one member, Gorbachev's use of the plural suggests that the chairman of the Military-Industrial Commission also regularly participated. In 1985 this was Yuriy Maslyukov; after 1988 it was Igor Belousov.

[7]Gorbachev statement in Yazov confirmation debate, July 3, 1989.

[8]Kryuchkov statement in *Pravda*, June 21, 1990.

1988 until the 1991 coup, Vladimir Kryuchkov) and even the head of Gosplan, the State Planning Commission.[9] There is strong reason to believe that none of these three latter positions—foreign minister, KGB chief, Gosplan head—had been given regular seats on the Defense Council in either the Khrushchev or the Brezhnev eras.[10] On the other hand, Gorbachev and Zaykov imply by omission that officials without functional national security responsibilities who were on the Defense Council at certain periods in the past—such as the second-ranking Central Committee secretary (until 1990, Gorbachev's conservative opponent Yegor Ligachev)—were now again excluded as Defense Council members.[11] In this respect, Gorbachev apparently continued a policy toward the ranking members of the Central Committee secretariat that Andropov had resumed in 1983 and had applied to Gorbachev himself.

The practical point of all these details is that in 1985 Gorbachev brought all the important national security interests and players together around one table, while significantly widening the definition of "national security" to include the foreign minister as well as an expanded group of key military figures. At the same time, Gorbachev managed to exclude those, however important politically, whose jobs did not involve national security matters.

One aspect of the way Gorbachev organized the Defense Council in 1985 was to prove particularly important to the Soviet military. This was the fact that he had admitted to the inner sanctum, where the procurement and deployment decisions most senstitive to the military were decided, one man—Shevardnadze—who during the five years that he remained there was to prove outspokenly critical of many past Defense Council decisions and consistently hostile to the military

---

[9] Statement in Zaykov interview in *Pravda*, November 27, 1989. The Gosplan head has an important national security function because of his role in the allocation of material resources for military industry.

[10] For the Khrushchev era, see Penkovskiy, *op. cit.* For the Brezhnev era, see Whitton, *op. cit.*, who provides evidence indicating that KGB Chairman Andropov did not become a member of the Defense Council until he left his KGB job in 1982. During the 1970s, the KGB head, like the service chiefs, had apparently participated in occasional council meetings on an *ad hoc* basis when his interests were directly involved.

[11] We have already seen from Penkovskiy's testimony that the two ranking members of the Central Committee secretariat after Khrushchev, Frol Kozlov and Mikhail Suslov, were active members of Khrushchev's Supreme Military Council. Neither had direct responsibility for military affairs. Whitton provides evidence that Brezhnev discontinued this practice between 1965 and 1973, but thereafter readmitted to his Defense Council the two ranking party secretaries (at that time, Suslov and Andrey Kirilenko).

leadership's view of Soviet military needs. This had never happened before.

On the other hand, the military apparently retained one traditional structural advantage in the workings of the Gorbachev Defense Council. This is the fact that

> without a sizeable [Defense Council] staff of its own, the tasks of setting the agenda of meetings, preparing briefings, and presenting options [fell] to the General Staff, which thereby [exerted] considerable influence thanks to its monopoly of military expertise.[12]

It is, however, unlikely—given Gorbachev's struggles with the military recounted below—that the General Staff was able to "set the agenda" for the Defense Council in the Gorbachev era. The General Staff role as Defense Council secretariat had in fact long been a sensitive point for the General Staff's relationship with the Politburo. Seweryn Bialer, relying on good personal sources in Moscow, has asserted that in Andropov's time—that is, during the period when then Chief of the General Staff Marshal Ogarkov was offering a persistent challenge to the political leadership[13]—serious consideration was given to changing the staffing system. Andropov, reports Bialer, "was said to have planned to establish an independent staff for the Defense Council, composed in part of civilian specialists on military, economic, and political questions, and in part of military specialists who would be permanently transferred to the Council from the Ministry of Defense and the General Staff. This could have offered him greater flexibility in dealing with proposals and requests from the armed forces."[14]

In fact, this did not happen, possibly because the change encountered too much political opposition, or possibly because Andropov died too soon. It will be seen, however, that the issue endured in Gorbachev's day, and was probably a central point of dispute in the crisis that arose over the Defense Council in the spring of 1990.

---

[12]Seweryn Bialer, *The Soviet Paradox*, Alfred A. Knopf, New York, 1986, p. 94. See also Kenneth Currie, "Soviet General Staff's New Role," *Problems of Communism*, March–April 1984, p. 39, who concurs that the General Staff provided secretariat staff functions for the Defense Council.

[13]See Harry Gelman, *Gorbachev and the Future of the Soviet Military Institution*, IISS Adelphi Paper No. 258, Spring 1991, pp. 9–10, 18.

[14]Bialer, *op. cit.*

THE FOUR BROAD DEFENSE COUNCIL FUNCTIONS

What did Gorbachev's Defense Council do? In broadest terms, according to Lev Zaykov, its job was "to implement supreme organizational, exeutive, and control functions on specific issues of the country's defense capacity and security and to coordinate the activities of the competent departments."[15]

Within this framework, traditionally the most basic function was decisionmaking on allocation of resources for development and procurement of major weapons systems. Thus, "with the involvement of major specialists, scientists, and designers,"[16] the Defense Council was said to "adopt and confirm" the "biggest strategic military programs."[17] In the last years of the Gorbachev era, as the economic constraints multiplied, Gorbachev's council was also increasingly obliged to make decisions about the selection of programs for reduction or deletion; and by the summer of 1989, according to Gorbachev, the council was engaged in a process that had already cut "dozens of programs."[18] As part of the same process, the Defense Council (along with other Soviet institutions) was supposed to help formulate policy regarding the "conversion" of some of the capacity of military industry to make nonmilitary goods.

As discussed later, one of the key symptoms of the eventual breakdown of the Defense Council machinery in the last year of the Soviet regime was the decay of the traditional ability of the regime to follow through with resources for the Defense Council's decisions regarding military programs. One factor that was to erode the Defense Council's power to put into effect the decisions it made on military resource allocation and funding was the deepening Soviet economic crisis. Another was the centrifugal diffusion of political power, which made all Soviet central institutions increasingly dependent on the financial cooperation of republic authorities.

Second, the Defense Council simultaneously evaluated "all possible consequences of our steps toward the reduction and limitation of weaponry and their influence on the overall balance of forces."[19] In the summer of 1990, Zaykov said that the council, "with the participa-

---

[15]Zaykov speech at 28th Party Congress, reported in *Pravda*, July 4, 1990.

[16]Lizichev, *op. cit.*

[17]Zaykov speech, *Pravda*, July 4, 1990.

[18]Gorbachev statement to Supreme Soviet, Moscow radio, August 1, 1989, FBIS-USSR, August 2, 1989, p. 50.

[19]Zaykov interview in *Pravda*, November 27, 1989.

tion of competent experts," had "elaborated" all the Soviet Union's "main military-political initiatives" of this kind up to that point. These included such unilateral decisions as the announcement or revocation of moratoria on nuclear tests, all unilateral force reduction measures and force deployment changes, and the outlines if not the details of all big new Soviet packages for mutual arms reduction.[20] According to Shevardnadze, such steps as his 1990 announcement of the unilateral withdrawal of all remaining Soviet tactical missiles from central Europe were made "on the basis of a document signed by the defense minister and the Chief of the General Staff."[21] Such documents evidently incorporated Defense Council decisions. Presumably, at least until the emasculation of the Politburo's power in 1990, such steps were subsequently also approved by the Politburo.

Third, the Defense Council oversaw the internal organization and deployment of the armed forces, including *inter alia* such matters as "mobilization readiness plans"[22] and draft and manpower policies. Thus, for example, according to Yazov, the Defense Council in March 1989 adopted a decision to stop drafting students; this decision was then published as a Supreme Soviet decree.[23] In the later stages of its existence, the council was obliged to decide such matters as how much money from its own budget the Defense Ministry would be forced to divert from other purposes to improve the living conditions of its officers.[24]

Since it presided over broad organizational questions, the Defense Council was responsible for reviewing and approving the new plans for reorganization of the forces as they were worked out by the General Staff, before they were submitted to the Supreme Soviet to be debated and enacted as legislation. This task was of course intimately interwoven with the first Defense Council task, that of approving long-term plans for hardware development and production. The future coup conspirator Oleg Baklanov, who between 1988 and 1990 was a Central Committee secretary responsible under Zaykov for

---

[20]*Ibid.* As will be seen below, however, this does not mean that in the Gorbachev era the Defense Council was where the details of the evolving Soviet negotiating position in arms control talks were coordinated.

[21]*Pravda*, June 26, 1990. Shevardnadze said this in response to a Soviet general who had publicly charged that he had thereby taken an initiative that "was not worked on in the Ministry of Defense." (Moscow Television, June 22, 1990, FBIS-USSR, June 26, 1990 p. 88.)

[22]*Pravda*, November 27, 1989.

[23]Yazov speech to Supreme Soviet, Moscow radio, July 3, 1989, FBIS-USSR *Daily Report,* July 5, 1989, p. 42.

[24]Gorbachev statement at Komsomol Congress, *Pravda*, April 12, 1990.

helping to supervise the planning of hardware development, thus alluded without elaboration in the summer of 1990 to recommendations he had "submitted for consideration to the Politburo and the Defense Council" on "highly important questions of military organizational development."[25]

And finally, the Defense Council decided Soviet strategy and doctrine, a function obviously closely linked with the organization and deployment of the armed forces. In 1989, during the Supreme Soviet debate over the confirmation of Defense Minister Yazov, Gorbachev emphasized the Defense Council's role as the sole source of Soviet military strategy. Critics of Yazov were wrong, Gorbachev said, to blame Yazov for alleged neglect of this question, for strategy was simply not his responsibility, but that of the council. He could and should participate in the council's debate on these matters—along with all the other members—but the council and only the council would decide.[26] Like much else that Gorbachev said on this occasion, his ostensible defense of Yazov was in fact a rather pointed way of emphasizing his intention of ensuring the subordination of the military to him. There had been several periods in the post-Stalin era when some military leaders had advanced a thinly veiled claim to a predominant military role in determining strategy.

In the process of changing the Soviet Union's strategy, Gorbachev first found it necessary to try to get the military leaders to agree to a fundamental shift in doctrine toward a "defensive" orientation. "First of all," he declared, "we had to look at what kind of doctrine we ought to be pursuing. That was what everything began with. A doctrine was formed, a military-political [sic] doctrine." This defensive doctrine, in turn, was to be the basis for the restructuring of the armed forces.[27]

In fact, getting the military to agree, even in principle, to this massive change in thinking required a process that was neither easy nor brief. It seems likely that one of the major reasons Gorbachev wanted the key military leaders present at the outset at sessions of his version of the Defense Council was because he wished to use the new council as a vehicle to force them to reorient their attitudes, on doctrine and on many other matters. Former Chief of the General Staff Akhromeyev

---

[25]Baklanov speech to 28th Party Congress, *Pravda*, July 7, 1990. In the spring of 1991, Baklanov gave up his Central Committee post to become First Deputy Chairman of the Defense Council, and in August 1991 he took part in the abortive coup attempt.

[26]*Pravda*, July 4, 1989.

[27]*Ibid.*

thus stated in the summer of 1989 that for two years—that is, from 1987 on—there had been an ongoing "discussion" in the Defense Council on the question of shifting traditionally offensively oriented Soviet military doctrine toward "a defensive variant."[28] As will be seen below, there are good reasons for believing that the debate was sharp, even acromonious.

THE MAIN MILITARY COUNCIL

A further aspect of the Defense Council's arrangements remains to be noted. From at least Khrushchev's time, a second and much larger body, the Main Military Council, existed as an adjunct to the Defense Council and its predecessors. Until recently there was almost no information available about this body, and there was considerable uncertainty about its functions and subordination. There is now sufficient evidence to conclude that it served as a grand assembly of all the important commanders in the Soviet armed forces, convened irregularly, that is, apparently only every few years,[29] to allow the chairman of the Defense Council—traditionally the party General Secretary and, after the spring of 1990 the president—and a few of his political colleagues to provide general guidance to the armed forces on special occasions. Generally, these occasions were turning points in the Soviet civil-military relationship.

After many years of official reticence, the Main Military Council of the Defense Council was identified publicly—and its function at last made clear—on an occasion when it was convened in the fall of 1989. At that time, Yazov and Gorbachev addressed the assembled officers on the "future development" of the armed forces, in a large gathering attended by "members and alternate members of the Politburo . . . , heads of defense industries and high-ranking officials of the party apparatus."[30] An earlier occasion when the Main Military Council is likely to have been convened was during Gorbachev's July 1985 visit to Minsk, when he, then Defense Minister Sokolov, and party secretary Zaykov met with an "assembly of high-ranking commanding offi-

---

[28]William E. Odom, "Soviet Military Doctrine," *Foreign Affairs*, Summer 1989, p. 130.

[29]Thus, Col. Gen. Boris Gromov, former commander of Soviet forces in Afghanistan and former commander of the Kiev Military District, revealed at the time of his appointment as First Deputy Minister of the Interior in December 1990 that he had only attended one meeting of the Main Military Council in his life. This was presumably the meeting announced in the fall of 1989. (Interview in *Dialog* (Moscow), No. 18, December 1990.)

[30]TASS, October 18, 1989.

cers," and when Gorbachev delivered an unpublished speech that apparently shocked the assembled officers by suggesting the need for radical change.[31]

Another occasion was almost certainly Brezhnev's final meeting with a large group of officers a month before he died in 1982, when he told them that they should not expect significantly greater resources, but must make greater efforts to translate the resources given them into heightened military capabilities.[32] Yet another convocation of the Main Military Council probably occurred in early April 1967, during the brief interval between Defense Minister Malinovskiy's death and the appointment of Marshal Grechko to replace him. The Soviet press reported that Brezhnev, President Podgornyy, and Premier Kosygin had met with a large group of the senior commanders, who heard Brezhnev talk "about certain questions of military development."[33]

In short, the Main Military Council does not seem to have been a working body, much less a decisionmaking body, but rather was evidently the party leader's vehicle for communicating directly with the broad senior officer corps on rare and unusual occasions, in effect over the heads of the top military leaders who sat on the Defense Council. It appears to have been convened only at those extraordinary junctures when the party leader (later, the USSR president) as Defense Council chairman deemed it necessary to convey a special message of particular importance. There is evidence that since at least the Khrushchev era[34] it served this function and was controlled by the chairman of the Defense Council rather than by the Minister of Defense.[35] The evidence also suggests, however, that this relation-

---

[31]TASS, July 10, 1985.

[32]*Pravda*, October 28, 1982.

[33]*Krasnaya Zvezda*, April 6, 1967.

[34]A Soviet biographer of Marshal Malinovskiy has claimed that in November 1957—that is, as soon as Malinovskiy had replaced Zhukov—"the Military Council attached to [*pri*] the Defense Council of the USSR was renamed the Main Military Council attached to the Defense Council of the USSR." (V. S. Golubovich, *Marshal R. Ya. Malinovskiy*, Voyenizdat, Moscow, 1984, p. 207.)

This statement would also appear to imply that during the Khrushchev era the Supreme Military Council of the USSR, the name cited by Penkovskiy, had already been retitled the Defense Council. It seems possible, however, that Golubovikch was anachronistically employing the usage of his own day in alluding to the council. In the absence of other evidence, I have continued to use Penkovskiy's version of the title of this institution when referring to the pre-Brezhnev period.

[35]The minister has subordinated to him, instead, an advisory body of senior ministry officials called the Collegium of the Ministry of Defense, which is entirely at his disposal and evidently meets far more frequently. See Edward L. Warner, Josephine

ship was reaffirmed and formalized at the time of Khrushchev's ouster of Defense Minister Zhukov in 1957 on charges of "bonapartism."[36]

Bonan, and Erma Packman, *Key Personnel and Organizations of the Soviet Military High Command*, RAND, N-2567-AF, April 1987.

[36]The timing strongly implies that the change cited in footnote 34 was a consequence of the Zhukov ouster, and was associated with other steps taken simultaneously to reinforce Khrushchev's ability to communicate directly with and to control the senior officer corps.

4. THE COMMISSION FOR ARMS CONTROL COORDINATION

Revelations in 1990 by Lev Zaykov made it clear that although it was the Defense Council that "elaborated" unilateral Soviet military inititiatives and "evaluated" the strategic consequences of arms control decisions, there was another powerful institution in the Gorbachev era that coordinated the evolving Soviet negotiating position in arms control talks. Within a year after Gorbachev took office, a "special commision was set up in the Politburo to this end," to deal with "the military and technical aspects of international politics, including preparations for talks on arms reductions."[1] This body was initially called, according to one insider, the "Political Commission."[2] The recommendations of this commission, according to Shevardnadze, were submitted to the political leadership.[3] After the emergence of the executive presidency and the decline in the significance of the party Politburo in 1990, the locus of Soviet political leadership changed, and the Political Commission for Arms Control, like the Defense Council, was shifted to become subordinate to Gorbachev in his capacity as president. It was then reportedly renamed the "Group on Negotiations."[4]

At the outset in 1986, Zaykov was made chairman of this Political Commission of the Politburo, but his fellow Politburo members Shevardnadze and Aleksandr Yakovlev—the two foreign policy radicals—were also placed on the commission by Gorbachev; these three were evidently the only full Politburo members on the commission. In addition, the commission, according to Zaykov, contained "leaders from the Defense Ministry, the KGB, the Military-Industrial Commission of the Council of Ministers [the VPK], and other departments." According to statements made privately by the senior military industrial leader Viktor Surikov after the collapse of the Soviet Union, there were seven members of the commission in all, and the

---

[1]Zaykov speech at 28th Party Congress, *Pravda*, July 4, 1990. A year earlier, Shevardnadze had revealed, without elaboration, the existence of a Politburo commission to "coordinate the formulation of positions at disarmament talks." (*Izvestiya* interview, March 23, 1989.) Zaykov implies, although he does not unequivocally state, that the commission was set up after January 1986.

[2]Rose Gottemoeller and Andrew Aldrin, Memorandum of Conversation with Viktor Surikov, January 27, 1992.

[3]*Pravda*, June 26, 1990.

[4]Gottemoeller and Aldrin.

four besides Zaykov, Shevardnadze, and Yakovlev were the defense minister, the chief of the General Staff, the chairman of the KGB, and the most senior military-industrial leader.[5]

THE COMMISSION'S "WORKING GROUP"

The commission, according to Zaykov, in turn had a "working organ," which was an "interdepartmental working group." Chaired by First Deputy Chief of the General Staff Col. Gen. Bronislav Omelichev, this group also had seven members, and apparently operated at the deputy minister level, including figures such as Deputy VPK Chairman Gennady Khromov and men of comparable rank from the KGB and foreign ministry.[6]

According to Zaykov, participants in the process run by this working group also included "representatives of other departments, scientists and experts from the USSR Academy of Sciences, and scientific research centers of the General Staff and of industry."[7] Most of these people were apparently not members of the working group itself, but members of a body of experts that met to support the working group.[8] In this connection, according to Zaykov, "a fundamental role was designated to the International Department of the Central Committee,"[9] and more "particularly" to the "Defense Department [of the Central Committee], in which a special subdivision for the issues of military policy was set up."[10] The future coup conspirator Oleg Baklanov, who as Central Committee secretary supervised the military-industrial work of the party Defense Department from 1988 on, stated in the summer of 1990 that he was "involved in preparing

---

[5]*Ibid*. Although, according to Surikov, he knew that during the last year of the Soviet Union this seat was held by presidential adviser Oleg Baklanov, it seems likely that during the first few years of the group's existence Baklanov was too junior for such a role, since he was then still only a minister. Initially, therefore, this military-industrial seat on the commission was probably held by the VPK chairman (at first Yuriy Maslyukov, after 1988 Igor Belousov).

[6]*Ibid*.

[7]*Pravda*, July 4, 1990.

[8]Gottemoeller and Aldrin.

[9]This was a change, for until Gorbachev's time the International Department had had little to do with defense matters. This new function of the International Department was signalled to the outside world by the 1986 appointment to the department of the former General Staff official Lt. Gen. Viktor Staradubov. Staradubov was widely believed at the time to be concerned with arms control issues. He was evidently named to the International Department to become its representative in the newly formed working group of the Politburo Commission on Arms Control.

[10]This, presumably, was why the name of this Central Committee department was then changed from "defense industry department."

the negotiating process,"[11] and Surikov has confirmed that Baklanov himself served as a member of the arms control commission's working group.[12]

This complex organizational arrangement, like that of the Gorbachev Defense Council, evidently built on precedents from earlier periods. In the 1970s, the West had heard persistent reports of the emergence of some mechanism in the Soviet regime for the interdepartmental coordination of SALT negotiating positions, and there were suggestions that this mechanism was "possibly in a special *ad hoc* group under the control of the Politburo or Secretariat."[13] Nevertheless, Zaykov's claim that the Gorbachev-era mechanism represented a fresh organizational start may be justified, since there was considerable evidence that the Soviet internal coordinating machinery had become atrophied during the period of policy paralysis and confusion in Brezhnev's last years and in the ensuing interregnum.

In any event, Gorbachev's new system for arms control policy coordination was apparently distinguished by the effort made to broaden the base of institutional representation, and also to provide at least marginally greater political firepower to views differing from those of the military. In both respects, the changes resembled those he was simultaneously making in the Defense Council.

This is not to deny that the military leadership from the start retained an extremely powerful position in the "working group" of the arms control commission, an organizational position which, as we shall see, was further strengthened in the last year of the Soviet Union. The military and its sympathizers from military industry—such as party secretary Baklanov—were obviously far more thickly represented at this level than the foreign ministry and its friends. Moreover, according to Shevardnadze, the delegations that negotiated with the West in the Gorbachev era were "staffed by the relevant departments on a parity basis,"[14] so that military officers and military-

---

[11]*Pravda*, July 7, 1990.

[12]Gottemoeller and Aldrin. According to Surikov, Baklanov at some stage was also a member of the commission itself, and thus served as a personal link to its lower-level staff organization. He seems unlikely to have played this dual role, however, before he became a junior Central Committee secretary in February 1988, and possibly not until considerably later.

[13]Douglas F. Garthoff, "The Soviet Military and Arms Control," *Survival*, Vol. 19, No. 6, November–December 1977, p. 246. Garthoff cites earlier prescient speculation to this effect by Matthew P. Gallagher and Karl F. Spielmann in *Soviet Decision-Making for Defense*, New York, Praeger, 1972, pp. 29–30.

[14]*Pravda*, June 26, 1990.

industrial officials taking part in the talks had ample opportunity to feed their views back through their respective departmental channels to the coordinating commission in Moscow.

In addition, as already noted, the labors of the "working group" were apparently being constantly second-guessed by the senior military from the vantage point of the Defense Council. Clearly, if one Soviet decisionmaking body "evaluated" the strategic implications of potential arms control concessions that were being considered for adoption by another Soviet policymaking entity, the first group's findings were likely to have a sizable impact on the second body's decision whether to make those concessions—particularly since, as we have seen, many of the same individuals were involved in both places.

Finally, as Shevardnadze has also revealed, the working group's "center for coordinating positions and elaborating directives" was the General Staff.[15] Shevardnadze evidently meant that the General Staff served as the working group's secretariat, staffing its coordination efforts and controlling the distribution of its documents and supporting information. This conclusion seems particularly safe inasmuch as a first deputy chief of the General Staff chaired the working group. As suggested earlier, this evidence also strongly implies that the General Staff continued under Gorbachev to serve precisely the same function for the Defense Council as well. So long as this relationship endured, the military leadership retained an important advantage in dealing with senior civilians.

THE TWO ADVERSE EFFECTS FOR THE MILITARY

Nevertheless, in two respects the new arrangement did represent an evolution of Soviet decisionmaking practice in a direction unwelcome to the military at least until 1990. First, at the working level, the proliferation of institutions and individuals authorized to participate in the inner discussion of the pros and cons of ongoing negotiations inevitably put some pressure on the General Staff to widen access to classified military information, which it had long sought to restrict rigidly so as to protect its own monopoly on the advisory use of such information. This trend, in turn, probably served as an opening wedge, legitimating to some degree the much wider public discussion of military issues that Gorbachev, Yakovlev, and Shevardnadze began to encourage from 1987 on, to the chagrin of the military leadership.

---

[15]*Ibid.*

More important, the makeup of the decisionmaking Politburo commission itself was surely unwelcome to the General Staff. The inclusion of Yakovlev as well as Shevardnadze—during the five years that they remained in place—substantially increased the political weight of the forces likely to endorse negotiating concessions in the commission's discussions. As will be seen, this equation was to change significantly during the last year of the commission's (and the Soviet Union's) existence, after Gorbachev temporarily moved to the right, Shevardnadze and Yakovlev departed, and Baklanov's role became magnified.

5. POLICY STRUGGLE IN THE TWO DECISIONMAKING ORGANS

Over the years of the Gorbachev regime, considerable evidence accumulated about the bitterness of the disputes that carried from issue to issue in the Defense Council, in the arms control commission, and in the commission's working group. Broadly speaking, these debates mostly centered on two closely related areas: the reform of the Soviet military institution and arms control concessions.

EARLY CONTENTION OVER PERSONNEL CHANGES

Initially, it was not arms control but Gorbachev's early effort to shake up the Ministry of Defense that seems to have generated the most heat within the Defense Council. This struggle began in earnest in December 1986, when Gorbachev took his first decisive step toward asserting his will over the military leadership by bringing General Dmitriy Yazov from the Far East to Moscow as deputy minister of defense in charge of personnel. Ironically enough, Yazov, who five years later was to join in the attempt to displace Gorbachev, was at the outset Gorbachev's key ally in the military establishment. It seems clear from Gorbachev's statements in 1989 that only after Yazov reached Moscow and took over the personnel function did Gorbachev find it possible to attempt to purge the Ministry of Defense on a systematic basis. At this juncture, Yazov showed himself, in Gorbachev's opinion, to be a "courageous and principled Communist." Although he was "far from successful in everything," he showed devotion to principle in attacking the corruption and "protectionism . . . which had literally put to rout many echelons of cadres."[1]

Acting at this time as Gorbachev's agent in a process that was strongly resented by many senior officers, Yazov as deputy minister for personnel prepared advisory memoranda for Gorbachev with recommendations on how to conduct the purge. Subsequently, after Yazov's elevation to be Minister of Defense, structural and institutional changes to eliminate deadwood on a wholesale basis apparently began to supplement the individual personnel shifts. According to one military-industrial leader, "Comrade Yazov, after having become minister, took decisive measures . . . to reduce the number of posts—

---

[1]Gorbachev statement in Yazov confirmation debate, July 3, 1989.

including some rather high ones—of military officers working in industry."²

Moreover, the pruning that Yazov carried out for Gorbachev was apparently applied to some units that were, at least nominally, part of the ground force table of organization. According to Gorbachev's statements in the summer of 1989, "the building of the Armed Forces had been such as to allow garrisons to be maintained in the country, with positions [*dolzhnosty*] assigned to them, without any need for them." He and Yazov had dealt with such cases by "painlessly" liquidating many "so-called divisions." Gorbachev asserted that the Yazov leadership of the Ministry of Defense had liquidated 101 such "simulated" divisions, without weakening the army. Gorbachev did not elaborate further on the nature of these "so-called" or "simulated" divisions,³ but made it clear that these pseudo-units, in his opinion, had only been "feeding troughs"—presumably, for senior officers.⁴

The Defense Council was important in these initial Gorbachev efforts to reform the military institution because it was both the instrument he used to assert himself and the focus for the expression of officers' resentment. The process he had begun, says Gorbachev, was difficult, "both in dealing with the generals and with others." Changing the military attitude was not easy, and although the military needed "radical reconstruction," this process proved "still more difficult" in the armed forces "than in society," and "a lot of people don't like it." In fact, he asserted,

> It was so painful that I began to receive information that the Defense Council and its chairman [that is, Gorbachev] were moving too sharply, and the Marshals requested me to bear this comment in mind.⁵

As time went on, this friction within the Defense Council over Gorbachev's campaign to change the military institution became in-

---

²V. L. Lapygin, address to Supreme Soviet of USSR, July 3, 1989, in stenographic report of that day's session.

³Both a Soviet transcript and a recording of his statement confirm that he used the word *divisii*.

⁴Gorbachev statement in Yazov confirmation debate, July 3, 1989. Although any interpretation must be speculative, it would appear that he was alluding to skeleton organizations of some kind existing largely but not entirely on paper, perhaps intended to be activated in the event of full-scale wartime mobilization after other low-category divisions were filled out.

⁵Paul Quinn-Judge, *Christian Science Monitor*, July 12, 1989. This Gorbachev assertion was excised from published Soviet versions of Gorbachev's comments.

creasingly exacerbated by friction over his evolving arms control policies.

THE KRASNOYARSK RADAR

A vivid example was the argument that apparently began at the outset of the Gorbachev regime and went on for four years behind the scenes in the Defense Council and the Politburo arms control commission over how to respond to American charges that the Krasnoyarsk radar tracking station was a violation of the Anti-Ballistic Missile (ABM) treaty. The Gorbachev leadership for a long time replied to this complaint with flat denials and mendacious assertions that the facility was intended to track satellites. Eventually, the Soviet leaders shifted, and tacitly admitted that the location and orientation of the Krasnoyarsk radar raised a legal problem, but were nevertheless only willing to remove this facility if the United States reciprocated with removal or modification of certain facilities of its own. And finally, in 1989, the Gorbachev leadership further retreated to an unqualified public admission that this installation was a violation of the treaty and a public pledge to dismantle it unilaterally.

One gets the flavor of the private Defense Council debate that accompanied this public evolution of the Soviet position from Shevardnadze's remarks at the last stage, in the fall of 1989. He asserts that the Soviet leaders had "investigated" the Krasnoyarsk facility "for four years," but that "the whole truth did not become known to the country's leadership right away." Only "eventually we were convinced: The station had not been constructed in a place where this could be done [according to the terms of the treaty]." Shevardnadze observes that

> throughout these years we were waging a struggle . . . to preserve the ABM Treaty as the foundation for strategic stability. We sought arguments and conducted a highly complex debate on interpretation of the treaty articles and appendices. And all the time this station on the scale of the Egyptian pyramids has stood, demonstrating, let us be frank, a breach of the ABM Treaty.[6]

Shevardnadze's half-hearted suggestion that the Gorbachev leadership required four years of "investigation" to discover that the Krasnoyarsk radar was not a satellite tracking station is obviously not credible. Even more important, Shevardnadze used language implying that he did not seriously expect or even wish this explanation

---

[6]*Ibid.*

to be believed, since he simultaneously alluded directly to the opposition to Soviet retreat on this issue which he had personally confronted in the Defense Council. Moreover, such opposition had been heard recently as well as in the past. Even after the Soviet leadership had discovered the truth, obstruction, previously encountered from someone, continued:

> Finally, we put an end to the problem. We stated that we were dismantling the station. Again, objections were raised—our interests were being abandoned, *people said*. (Emphasis added.)

THE STRUGGLE OVER INF

Another case in which we now have evidence of long, tortuous dispute within the Soviet decisionmaking organs was that of the Intermediate-range Nuclear Forces (INF) Treaty. It seems likely that much of the erratic backing and filling that Gorbachev displayed during the INF negotiations—especially by withdrawing, reimposing, and again withdrawing attempted links to the French and British nuclear systems and to the Strategic Defense Initiative (SDI)—was influenced by the internal coordination process and represented his attempt to demonstrate to a captious unseen audience in the decisionmaking organs that additional concessions could not be obtained by returning to Soviet negotiating demands that had already been abandoned.

It now seems clear that the military views expressed in the Defense Council and the Political Commission for Arms Control were themselves divided over the acceptability of destroying many more missiles than NATO was required to do under the "zero option." A senior Strategic Rocket Forces general who says that he had favored accepting this unfavorable ratio of missiles to be sacrificed—on the ground that it was worth it "to get rid of the threat of Pershings which could pierce us . . . to the Volga"—has alluded to the opposition of unnamed military colleagues. These generals, he asserts, had thought only in terms of one "strategic variant: the USA less, the USSR more," and had therefore sought to "persuade us that this treaty mustn't be accepted, that this nearly spelled the end of our defense."[7]

Shevardnadze has similarly alluded to "sharp disputes" in the "multitude of consultations among military and civilian experts" during the preparation of the INF Treaty. Different sides in the coordi-

---

[7] Col. Gen. Igor Sergeyev, deputy commander of the Strategic Rocket Forces, interviewed in *Moscow News*, No. 8–9, March 11–18, 1990.

nation process had their "own perception of ways to ensure statewide interests," he said, and consequently, "not all the specialists" —presumably, in the working group of the Political Commission— "immediately supported the idea that was put forward."[8] Indeed, in the course of the INF negotiations, according to Shevardnadze, "there were quite a few people who accused the diplomats of making concessions and giving ground and not taking defense interests into account."[9]

There was also considerable acrimony within the defense establishment itself, particularly when the shorter-range SS-23 was added to the list of weapons to be eliminated under the INF agreement. Four years after the negotiations, one officer asserted that then Ground Forces commander Army General Yevgeniy Ivanovskiy, "as a token of protest, refused to sign off on the agreed document on destroying the missiles," and as a result did not get an expected posting in the General Staff.[10] Subsequently, the Ground Forces, for reasons explored below, emerged as a strong center of resistance within the military establishment to the next stage of arms control, and also to fundamental reform of the armed forces. Indeed, Ivanovskiy's successor as Ground Forces commander, Army General V. A. Varennikov, was to become heavily involved in the attempted coup of August 1991.

THE STRUGGLE OVER CONVENTIONAL FORCE REDUCTION

The argument over INF that went on in the Soviet decisionmaking bodies during 1986 and 1987 led by degrees into the even more difficult internal struggle over conventional force reduction. This struggle evidently commenced in earnest in the autumn of 1987, and the

---

[8]Shevardnadze interview, *Izvestiya*, March 23, 1989. After the demise of the Soviet Union, the military-industrial official Viktor Surikov confirmed that there had also been recurring differences among the military-industrial organizations represented in the working group of the Political Commission for Arms Control. (Gottemoeller and Aldrin.)

[9]*Pravda*, October 24, 1989.

[10]*Krasnaya Zvezda*, November 13, 1991 (FBIS-SOV, November 15, 1991, pp. 1–4). Ivanovskiy was apparently infuriated because his institutional interests had not been protected in the coordination process. The SS-20, the main subject of the INF talks, was subordinated to the Strategic Rocket Forces, which were heavily involved in the internal discussion that approved the INF decisions. However, the SS-23, a relatively late addition to the agreement, was subordinated not to the SRF but to a Missile Forces and Artillery Directorate of the Ground Forces establishment, which was allegedly not apprised of the decision to eliminate this weapon until after the decision was taken.

issues involved transcended arms control and the fate of the future Conventional Forces in Europe (CFE) treaty.

There were several reasons why this dispute proved particularly protracted and traumatic. With the fall of the East European empire in 1989, the external geopolitical environment that was the original backdrop for Soviet agreement with the West on mutual conventional force reduction drastically changed during the CFE negotiations, to the Soviet Union's marked disadvantage. Meanwhile, with the growth in the strength of Soviet conservatives in 1990, the internal political environment in the Soviet Union also changed, for the time being, to the disadvantage of those Soviet leaders who favored CFE and to the advantage of those in the military who wished to try to renegotiate the agreement. On the other hand, despite the temporary improvement that now occurred in the military position in the Defense Council and the arms control coordinating commission between the fall of 1990 and the spring of 1991, the centrifugal process in the Soviet Union and the deterioration of the economy willy-nilly continued to press the Soviet national security decisionmakers in the direction of much smaller forces.

Most fundamentally, the question of reducing conventional forces become interwoven after 1987 with fundamental and unresolved questions about the future structure and role of the Soviet armed forces and future control of the decisionmaking organs.

SHEVARDNADZE'S ATTACK ON PAST DEFENSE COUNCIL DECISIONS

In retrospect, Gorbachev's decision in early 1987 to move more decisively toward an INF agreement proved to be a turning point for the position of the Soviet military institution in the Gorbachev era. Because one major decision taken by the Brezhnev Defense Council—the deployment of the SS-20s—was now being completely undone, the frame of reference that had produced that decision now became politically vulnerable. The tensions over military influence and the military's strategic preferences that had up to now been reflected primarily in arguments inside Gorbachev's decisionmaking bodies henceforth spread to the public domain. Gorbachev, Yakovlev, and Shevardnadze from this point on helped to encourage the gradual emergence of both civilian criticism of military institutions and civilian competition with the General Staff in the analysis of strategic matters.

This offensive began soon after Gorbachev's February 1987 decision to abandon for good the attempt he had made at Reykjavik to recreate a link between an INF settlement and SDI concessions. Although further mutual INF concessions would subsequently be required, the Soviet February climbdown was the decisive turning point leading toward agreement on the INF Treaty. At this juncture, the journalist Aleksandr Bovin for the first time publicly asked why the decision to deploy the SS-20 missiles had been made and how it could possibly have been justified.[11] Subsequently, once the INF Treaty was agreed upon, Bovin's Foreign Ministry supporters were in a position to pursue more directly the issue he had raised. In November, Deputy Foreign Minister Bessmertnykh—who three years later was to replace Shevardnadze—seized on the SS-20 question to make a pioneering complaint about past Defense Council performance.[12]

That Foreign Minister Shevardnadze stood behind his deputy on this matter was made abundantly clear the following summer. Four months before Gorbachev's December 1988 public UN announcement of unilateral Soviet force withdrawals and force reductions, Shevardnadze took his struggle against the General Staff out of the Defense Council and into the public arena. Shevardnadze came out into the open at a large Foreign Ministry conference in late July 1988 attended by much of the country's senior national security elite. There he launched a vehement public campaign against the status and interests of the General Staff, centering on a scathing indictment of specific instances of military-industrial and deployment decision-making by members of the past and present Defense Council. Shevardnadze also advanced the unprecedented demand that henceforth, "major innovations in defense development should be verified at the Ministry of Foreign Affairs to determine whether they correspond juridically to existing international agreements and to stated political positions."[13] On the face of it, this would appear to be a claim for a right of personal veto for the foreign minister over the defense-industrial programs presented by the Ministry of Defense and its various allies to the Defense Council. It is evident, however, that this extraordinary demand was never satisfied in the Gorbachev era.

---

[11]*Moscow News*, No. 10, March 15–22, 1987. A General Staff official made a polemical reply. (*Moscow News*, No. 11, March 23–29, 1987.) This was an epoch-making precedent, since explicit public polemics over Defense Council decisions regarding weapons deployment had never occurred before. Such polemics were to be repeated many times in the years to come.

[12]*New Times*, No. 46, November 23, 1987.

[13]*International Affairs*, No. 10, October 1988, p. 19.

THE COUNCIL DEBATE AND THE SHIFT TOWARD REDUCTIONS

At the moment Shevardnadze opened this public campaign in the summer of 1988, the Politburo and Defense Council had for nearly a year[14] been painfully inching toward their threefold decision: that is, the decision to make highly asymmetrical or unilateral force reductions, to begin significant reductions in the military budget, and to prepare for a major reorganization of the Soviet armed forces, supposedly to reorient them in a more defensive posture.

In the fall of 1987, Shevardnadze's allies in the press evidently were privately encouraged by Shevardnadze and Yakovlev to seize the opportunity created by the turn taken in the Defense Council discussion and to begin to prepare the way publicly for both asymmetrical and unilateral reductions. In October 1987, the well-connected institutchik Vitaliy Zhurkin and two colleagues published a pathbreaking article in which they said that "it would be a mistake to regard the bilateral process of reducing armaments as the only possible way." Zhurkin and his associates recalled the massive Khrushchev troop cuts of the 1950s, and claimed that "these unilateral measures, despite their scale . . . by no means weakened the international position of the USSR," but instead had strengthened Soviet prestige, influence, and security.[15]

The most intransigent of the military leaders saw the publication of these and other similar statements as ominous events. They evidently interpreted the leeway now being given to Shevardnadze's academic friends outside the Defense Council as evidence that Gorbachev intended to override the resistance inside the Council. From this perspective, the perennial Western debate how about how much "influence" these academics possessed was now beside the point. The mere fact that they were now encouraged to raise the previously forbidden topic of unilateral cuts was itself evidence that this issue had already reached an advanced stage in the internal debate in the decisionmaking organs.

This effort by a faction within the decisionmaking group to reach outside to manipulate public pressure to try to influence internal de-

---

[14]For discussion of the evidence regarding this process, see H. Gelman, *The Soviet Military Leadership and the Question of Deployment Retreats*, RAND, R-3664-AF, November 1988.

[15]Vitaliy Zhurkin, Sergey Karaganov, and Andrey Kortunov, "Reasonable Sufficiency—Or How to Break the Vicious Circle," *New Times*, No. 40, October 12, 1987.

cisionmaking, a phenomenon familiar in the West, was a revolutionary development in the Soviet Union, where until Gorbachev's time the leaders had sought to keep the national security decisionmaking process hermetically sealed from contamination by public opinion. After these hesitant beginnings in late 1987, this new tendency to use public opinion as a weapon in the internal decisionmaking debate was to become far more pronounced. With the radical diffusion of political power and the growth of pluralistic self-expression in the Soviet Union, it eventually became customary in Moscow as in Western capitals for decisionmakers with opposing interests to try to mobilize polemical pressure from allies outside all decisionmaking bodies to reinforce their desires inside those bodies.[16]

In early 1988, the most outspoken of the senior officers who protested against the implications of the fact that Zhurkin and company were now being allowed to praise unilateral reductions was Deputy Defense Minister and Air Defense Forces commander Army General Ivan Tretyak. In late February 1988, Tretyak warned in a dramatic interview that the Khrushchev troop cuts of the late 1950s had been disastrous for the Soviet Union—a "rash" step that "dealt a terrible blow at our defense capacity." He demanded that "any changes in our army should be considered a thousand times before they are decided upon."[17] A year later, after the reductions materialized, Tretyak was to violate party discipline by publicly protesting the major cut he said had been imposed on his service.[18]

Vociferous opposition within the high command to unilateral force reductions or withdrawals by no means ceased even after the General Staff in midsummer began "preparatory work on the decision to cut 500,000 men."[19] Moreover, despite heightened discussion of defense and endless talk about the new Soviet defensive doctrine, the bulk of senior military opinion seems to have remained entrenched in defense of the offense, even as the General Staff toiled for Gorbachev preparing successive draft versions of a troop cut that would supposedly demonstrate Soviet devotion to "defensive defense" and prepare

---

[16]One of many examples that might be cited of this phenomenon in national security decisionmaking was the question of nuclear testing, and the intense public agitation that arose in Kazakhstan in 1990–1991 over the continued use of the Semipalitinsk nuclear test site.

[17]*Moscow News*, No. 8, February 28–March 6, 1988.

[18]See the discussion in H. Gelman, T*he Soviet Turn Toward Conventional Force Reduction: The Internal Struggle and the Variables at Play*, RAND, R-3876-AF, December 1989, pp. 49–50. Tretyak was one of the officers immediately dismissed after the 1991 coup attempt.

[19]Akhromeyev interview in *La Republica* (Rome), March 11, 1989.

the way for a subsequent mutual conventional force reduction agreement.

The late Chief of the General Staff Akhromeyev later stated that "throughout the second half of 1988" the process of working out the unilateral reduction continued in the General Staff under the supervision of the Defense Council. He explained that

> in the Defense Council we made many reports, but suggestions were made to us, the military men, to work a bit more, to make things more precise, because it is a very complex matter.[20]

It seems evident that as this iterative process went on in the summer and fall, the General Staff was being dragged incrementally not only toward larger reductions, but toward reductions of a kind that would imply reorganization on principles many in the General Staff still found anathema.[21] Meanwhile, Shevardnadze's reaction as he listened to Akhromeyev's successive proposals for reductions in the Defense Council was reflected in a public statement made in early November to a Foreign Ministry gathering, where Shevardnadze asserted that "we are overdue in drafting and firming up a military doctrine and in imparting to it a strictly defensive emphasis."[22] Later, after the troop cut decision had been announced, and after Akhromeyev had been replaced as chief of the General Staff, his successor Moiseyev in effect acknowledged that Shevardnadze's charges had been quite correct.[23]

---

[20]Akhromeyev interview on Moscow television, October 9, 1989 (FBIS-SOV, October 13, 1989, p. 98). Although the defense industry official Viktor Surikov four years later claimed that Gorbachev merely rubber-stamped the arms control recommendations of the military-industrial complex, on Akhromeyev's testimony alone this was obviously not the case with the force reduction issue in the summer of 1988. (Gottemoeller and Aldrin.) As earlier suggested, Surikov's generalization may have had more substance in the fall of 1990.

[21]Four years later, a former senior GRU [Chief Administration for Intelligence] official revealed that Akhromeyev in 1988 had hedged against the tank reductions he was being compelled to make not only by diverting large numbers of tanks beyond the Urals, but also by demanding that the Soviet mobilization program be upgraded to give military industry a "surge capacity" to make 55,000 tanks a year. (Vitaliy Shlykov interview in *Yomiuri Shimbun*, October 25, 1991.)

[22]*Vestnik Ministerstva Inostrannykh Del*, No. 22, December 1, 1988.

[23]The General Staff, Moiseyev asserted, had indeed been tardy and had "dragged feet" in carrying out the "practical implementation of the requirements of a defensive military doctrine." In fact, he said, "we are only just beginning to tackle a series of questions, and some problems have not yet been properly approached." (*Krasnaya Zvezda*, February 10, 1989.)

It is evident that despite Marshal Akhromeyev's important services to Gorbachev in some arms control fora, Akhromeyev himself bore central responsibility for the General Staff's recalcitrance. The reason for this behavior seems plain from Akhromeyev's statements after his retirement in December 1988 to become a Gorbachev "adviser." Not only did he lack confidence in the notion of a "defensive defense," but more important, he was adamantly opposed to the early, large-scale reorganization of the armed forces that was implied if one took that notion seriously. Nine months after his removal, he asserted frankly that given the "billions of rubles" that had been invested in the existing Soviet military structure, and given the scope of the threat to the USSR that he saw continuing, "to change the structure now is, in my view, inexpedient."[24] Presumably, this is the position he had taken privately in Defense Council debates ever since Gorbachev in 1987 began to press the Defense Council to change Soviet doctrine. More broadly, he believed that many of the changes Gorbachev had begun would be disastrous for the military institution. Twenty months after his removal as chief of the General Staff, his intransigent opposition to what was happening to the Soviet army and to the Soviet state led him to take his life when the anti-Gorbachev coup failed.

THE BREAKDOWN OF THE COORDINATION MACHINERY OVER CFE

In late 1989 and early 1990, when—in the wake of the loss of Eastern Europe—Soviet negotiating concessions for the first time began to come under heavy attack from Soviet civilian and military conservatives, Shevardnadze and Zaykov became concerned to stress the collectivity of the security decisions reached. Both men emphasized that the military had consented in writing to those decisions, and praised the existence of what Shevardnadze called the "smoothly running mechanism for the coordination of positions, in which representatives of the party Central Committee, the government, the Defense Ministry, the KGB, the defense industry and scientists and diplomats work in close and creative collaboration. . . ."[25]

By the fall of 1990, however, this coordination system was in fact breaking down. Shevardnadze and the Foreign Ministry were by then being attacked more and more unmercifully by civilian and mili-

---

[24]Interview on Moscow television, October 9, 1989 (FBIS-SOV, October 13, 1989, p. 98).

[25]Shevardnadze speech to Supreme Soviet, *Pravda*, October 24, 1989.

tary reactionaries for concessions alleged to have contributed to the collapse of the Soviet position in Eastern Europe. Gorbachev, under increasing personal pressure, retreated on this front as on many others, and declined to defend Shevardnadze over policy decisions for which Gorbachev himself bore the primary responsibility. This disloyal Gorbachev behavior eventually contributed to Shevardnadze's decision, in December, to resign.

The CFE Treaty was bound up in this sequence of events because of the disastrous military implications of the loss of Eastern Europe, which by the fall of 1990 rendered the Soviet military leadership increasingly unhappy with the terms they had already accepted for the treaty. This discontent was apparently exacerbated by the manner in which negotiations were completed.

General Staff representatives, who were always present as part of the Soviet delegation in the regular CFE negotiations in Vienna, were apparently absent during the final bilateral talks between Shevardnadze and Secretary Baker in New York in early October that opened the way for the signing of the treaty in November. Senior military officials soon thereafter complained, not only privately but publicly, about certain of the concessions Shevardnadze had made without their participation in his New York session with Baker. In the six weeks between that Baker-Shevardnadze meeting and the treaty signing, the General Staff apparently contended in the Coordination Commission that Shevardnadze had unilaterally committed the Soviet Union on points that had not previously been agreed to by the military—in violation of the principle of collective responsibility.

This conflict in a decisionmaking organ over an arms control issue took place in precisely the period when Gorbachev was himself coming under massive attack because of his inability to halt the trend toward Soviet internal disintegration. The result was made visible when the CFE Treaty was signed in November 1990. It then became evident that if the General Staff had reluctantly agreed to the terms of the treaty, it had exacted a sizable price in the Soviet decisionmaking process.

To be sure, part of that price had already been collected in advance by the military leadership. As a hedge against the asymmetrical effects of the CFE Treaty, the General Staff had long since insisted on the large-scale redeployment of weapons east of the Urals before the treaty went into effect, to reduce the quantity of weapons subject to the treaty limits. This decision, which was carried out in 1989 and 1990,[26] had surely been confirmed in the Defense Council at the outset—that is, by early 1989 at the latest—in principle if not in detail. Moreover, its implementation in any case required extensive coordination within different branches of the government, in view of the economic consequences for the rail net.[27] The broad nature of what was being done was therefore necessarily known in advance by both Gorbachev and Shevardnadze, although the latter was probably not happy with the decision and may never have been conversant with the details.[28]

In addition, during the autumn of 1990, in discussions in the leadership's arms control coordinating commission, the General Staff evidently again prevailed over Shevardnadze to win Gorbachev's agreement to present to the West in November a reinterpretation of the Soviet force structure in Europe that redefined three motorized rifle divisions into categories exempting their weaponry from the treaty reductions. Gorbachev's consent to this strange last-minute behavior, which he well knew would endanger the treaty's ratification by the United States, was good evidence of the changing political atmosphere in Moscow in November 1990. This episode was also vivid evidence of a decline in the ability that Shevardnadze and his ministry had demonstrated a year earlier—in the fight over the Krasnoyarsk radar—to override military desires within the Defense Council and the arms control commission.

In the aftermath, however, the General Staff's CFE victory over the Foreign Ministry in the fall of 1990 proved ephemeral, because the United States and other Western states would not accept the last-minute Soviet actions as a basis for treaty ratification. During the six months between November 1990 and April 1991, this adamant Western stand apparently evoked a further struggle within the Soviet decisionmaking elite over how far to yield to Western pressure. In the course of this struggle, the Soviet military leaders, including Yazov, increasingly aired publicly their long-standing doubts and misgivings about the treaty, shedding the remainder of the inhibitions previously

---

[26]Statement by Maj. Gen. V. Manilov in *Sovetskaya Rossiya*, January 5, 1991.

[27]Antimilitary radicals have charged that the usurpation of much of Soviet rail capacity to transport these large quantities of weapons to the Urals in 1990 contributed significantly to the food distribution problems the country encountered. Some conservatives, while justifying the weapons movement, have acknowledged that it did have this effect. (*Sovetskaya Rossiya*, January 9, 1991.)

[28]In December 1990, when confronted by the United States with evidence of what had happened, Shevardnadze is said to have asserted privately that "they"—meaning the military—had been "lying to me." (*Financial Times*, January 15, 1991.)

imposed by the principle of collective responsibility. In the upshot, Gorbachev was unwilling to sacrifice the treaty, and therefore dispatched General Moiseyev to Washington in May 1991 to renegotiate the points at issue.[29] In the end, a compromise was reached in which certain face-saving provisions covered what was essentially a General Staff defeat.

This protracted story coincided with what was evidently a period of organizational changes and major personnel shifts within the Political Commission for Arms Control. This body was transferred from subordination to the Politburo to subordination to the presidency when Gorbachev became executive president in March 1990, and was then renamed the "Group on Negotiations." By the end of the year, it had lost the two leading figures who had created the most difficulty for the military, Shevardnadze and Yakovlev. Although Shevardnadze's replacement as foreign minister, Oleg Bessmertnykh, took his chair in the commission, and although Yakovlev was replaced by the presidential adviser Yevgeniy Primakov, the balance of power in the commission was obviously affected by the much weaker political status—and weaker convictions—of the two replacements. At the same time, the coloration of the renamed commission was to be increasingly influenced by the rise in the role played by the intransigent military-industrial apparatchik Oleg Baklanov, discussed below.

The subsequent history of the arms control coordination mechanism is interwoven with the story of the atrophy of all the decisionmaking machinery of the Soviet state in its final year. Particularly important in this connection was the final struggle over the Defense Council, to which we now turn.

---

[29]This step followed a precedent established with Moiseyev's predecessor, Marshal Akhromeyev. Shevardnadze has asserted that during the INF negotiations, he himself insisted to Gorbachev that Akhromeyev be brought in to participate personally with Shevardnadze and Gorbachev in dealing with the West at "the most crucial stages of the negotiations." Akhromeyev could thus be compelled to assume a share of personal responsibility for "the most crucial decisions" in the INF process, and with Akhromeyev's commitment once obtained, the objections of other institutions and personalities in the supporting decisionmaking apparatus could be bypassed or overridden.

This co-option of Akhromeyev for a direct role in arms control negotiations was of course seen not only in the INF talks, but also in other venues, notably in various stages of the START negotiations. Akhromeyev's prominent and authoritative role in the Reykjavik summit conference of late 1986 is well known. Although the surprise package presented to the United States on that occasion was no doubt carefully elaborated in advance in the Politburo commission, during the Reykjavik talks Akhromeyev displayed an impressive readiness to make what appeared to be spontaneous, *ad hoc* decisions committing the Soviet military establishment on points that may not have been previously coordinated in the Politburo commission.

6. THE LAST PHASE OF THE SOVIET STATE AND THE DECLINE OF CENTRAL SECURITY DECISIONMAKING

THE MARCH 1990 STRUGGLE OVER THE DEFENSE COUNCIL

In retrospect, it now seems clear that by the time Gorbachev in the summer of 1989 decided to make unprecedented revelations about the way he had organized the Defense Council up to that point, the circumstances underpinning those arrangements were already beginning a profound change.

At the Supreme Soviet session where he made those revelations, Gorbachev said that in the autumn of 1989, the next session of the Congress of People's Deputies would "form and set up" and "confirm" a "new Defense Council."[1] However, this did not happen. Six months later, in February 1990, the central military newspaper *Krasnaya Zvezda* recalled that selection of a Defense Council had indeed been included in the announced agenda of the Congress in the fall, but that the question for some unknown reason had been dropped. *Krasnaya Zvezda* also quoted one legislator as noting that promised legislation to formalize and govern the status of the Defense Council and the Main Military Council still had not been drafted.[2]

In view of what transpired soon thereafter, it is probable that more than sloth and inefficiency were responsible for this failure to act. By the winter of 1989, Gorbachev had evidently decided that public ratification of the membership and functions of the existing Defense Council would be inappropriate because he was now considering changes in the defense decisionmaking arrangements which he anticipated might cause political difficulties. Having resolved to create an executive presidency for himself, he knew he would be obliged to do something about the provision of the Brezhnev Constitution that gave responsibility for "forming" the Defense Council to the Presidium of the Supreme Soviet—which he would no longer head. Gorbachev evidently hoped to use the opportunity to revise the military decisionmaking process to strengthen his control over it, and he had reason to

---

[1] Gorbachev response to Supreme Soviet questions, Moscow Television, August 1, 1989 (FBIS-SOV, August 2, 1989, p. 50).

[2] *Krasnaya Zvezda*, February 15, 1990.

expect that this effort would stimulate behind-the-scenes resistance from the military.

The creation of the position of an executive president who would be invested with chairmanship of the Defense Council had been formally proposed by the leadership more than a year before, in constitutional amendments first put forward as early as the fall of 1988.[3] When Gorbachev finally decided to move to establish the presidential institution in early 1990, these draft constititutional amendments—in the version under consideration in February—provided that the new president would be "supreme commander of the Soviet Armed Forces and chairman of the USSR *Security and Defense* Council."[4] (Emphasis added.) The new name put forward for the council at this stage reflected the desire of certain key Gorbachev advisers—especially Academician Yevgeniy Velikhov—to have Gorbachev seize the occasion of the formal resubordination of the Defense Council from the Supreme Soviet to the executive presidency in order to change the Defense Council in two ways.

In the first place, as Velikhov explained to the Supreme Soviet,[5] he wished its function to be broadened to include internal security as well as external defense matters, hence the proposed change in title. Although he did not say so, this change alone would have necessarily enlarged the responsibilities of whatever secretariat served the council to cover matters beyond the purview of the General Staff, the traditional secretariat for the Council. Furthermore, Velikhov wished the new body to be modelled on the U.S. National Security Council, which, of course, has its own staff apparatus, largely civilian, to serve as its secretariat. These two changes, he said, were needed to make it possible to carry out a full reform of the Soviet military. In point of fact, they would together have gone a long way toward implementing the aborted proposal put forward in Andropov's time, to remove the General Staff as the secretariat of the Defense Council and to substitute a new, primarily civilian apparatus directly under the Soviet leader.

By early March, however, about a week before Gorbachev became president, the draft amendments to the Constitution to create the

---

[3] *New York Times*, October 22, 1988.

[4] *Asahi Shimbun*, February 24, 1990, which provided a leaked draft of the entire text of the proposed amendments in the version under consideration as of that date.

[5] Moscow central television, Februry 28, 1990 (FBIS-SOV, March 9, 1990), cited by Elizabeth Teague, "Membership of Presidential Council Announced," *RL Reports*, March 26, 1990.

presidency had been altered to delete all reference in the Constitution to a Defense Council in any guise. Instead, the new amendments provided for the creation of a Presidential Council under the president to "elaborate measures to implement the main directions of the USSR's domestic and foreign policy and ensure the country's security."[6] On the day these amendments were approved by the Congress of People's Deputies, the chairman of the Constitution drafting commission, Vladimir Kudryavtsev, told the Congress quite flatly that the Presidential Council would replace the Defense Council, which, he declared, was being "liquidated."[7]

A few days later, on March 15 and 16, Gorbachev and chief of the General Staff Moiseyev separately commented on this decision. At a press conference, Gorbachev was confronted by a journalist who explicitly asked why the Defense Council had been disbanded and was being replaced by the Presidential Council. In reply, Gorbachev did not contradict the premise and strongly implied that it was correct, saying that "a considerable proportion of those people who had been involved in the work of the Defense Council will continue to take part and assist the president in resolving those questions." He did not make clear how they would render this assistance, since only a few of them could be members of the Presidential Council. It is conceivable that Gorbachev was toying with the notion of creating a more informal support mechanism for defense decisionmaking than had previously existed, to be attached either to the Presidential Council or to the presidential office directly. In either case, the hold of the General Staff over the staffing machinery might be significantly weakened. The journalist also inquired as to how the Defense Council had "failed to please," but this question Gorbachev ignored.[8]

On the day after this press conference, Moiseyev published an interview in *Krasnaya Zvezda* in which he confirmed that it was his understanding that the Defense Council had indeed been abolished. Moiseyev complained that neither he nor any other military representative had been allowed [by Gorbachev and his agents] to participate in the debate in the legislature before the deed was done. He thus made it abundantly clear that the change had not been coordinated with the General Staff. Moiseyev went on to speak in terms that took for granted that the Presidential Council itself—and not any appara-

---

[6]*Izvestiya,* March 6, 1990.

[7]Moscow central television, March 13, 1990 (FBIS-SOV, March 14, 1990, p. 53). See Elizabeth Teague, footnote 5.

[8]*Pravda,* March 17, 1990.

tus subordinate to it—would, in fact, replace the Defense Council. Accordingly, he proposed that the Constitution be further amended to spell out for the Presidential Council a long list of specified functions that had previously belonged to the Defense Council, including its wartime conversion into a State Committee for the Defense of the USSR.[9]

However, as Gorbachev's appointments to the Presidential Council emerged in the next few weeks, it became apparent that many of the Presidential Council members, chosen by Gorbachev for reasons of political balance and expediency from diverse walks of life, knew little of military affairs. On the other hand, some key Defense Council members—such as Zaykov and Moiseyev—were not appointed to the Presidential Council. It was thus obvious that whatever Moiseyev had anticipated, this body was quite unsuited to replace the Defense Council. It seems very likely that this circumstance evoked private recriminations between Gorbachev and the military leadership, who attached great importance to coherence in the chain of command and the defense decisionmaking structure, and who certainly were unwilling to accept tamely the dilution of their own role implied by Gorbachev's actions.

Whatever took place behind the scenes between mid-March and mid-April, at the end of this period Gorbachev retreated.[10] On April 11, he manufactured an occasion to refer publicly to the Defense Council as an ongoing institution,[11] despite the fact that only four weeks earlier he had removed Brezhnev's mention of the council from the Soviet Constitution while rejecting Velikhov's proposal to create a new constitutional basis for its existence. The April 1990 Gorbachev retreat on the Defense Council issue in the face of pressure from the military-industrial complex was to foreshadow his more drastic retreat before such pressure later that year.

---

[9]*Krasnaya Zvezda*, March 16, 1990.

[10]It should be noted that immediately thereafter, Gorbachev began to make other visible concessions to the military. On April 29, Defense Minister Yazov was given a marshal's star, despite repeated indications in previous years that Gorbachev was determined to make no more promotions to that rank. And on May 1, the military were once again permitted to hold parades, after several years of denial.

[11]In responding to questions at a Komsomol congress, Gorbachev said that the Defense Council "operates under the President," and that a program to improve the living conditions of Soviet officers would be examined "by the government, the Defense Council, and the Presidential Council." (*Pravda*, April 12, 1990.)

THE COUNCIL REVIVES AS GORBACHEV MOVES TO THE RIGHT

At the end of May—six weeks after Gorbachev's reversal regarding the Defense Council—a General Staff official, Major General G. V. Zhivitsa,[12] insisted that "the President and the Defense Council" were indeed "working out the basic directions of military development." Moreover, this senior officer indicated that a major reorganization of the Defense Council had by now taken place, at least on paper. "Today," he said, "the circle of persons who form this Council has been determined. Many of the former members of the Defense Council do not belong to it. For example, the commanders of the armed services."[13]

However, despite Gorbachev's pointed allusion to the Defense Council in April, and despite the General Staff's testimony about Defense Council reorganization, high-level doubt seems to have persisted until late summer about Gorbachev's willingness to follow through on what he had said in April—that is, on his readiness to resume using the council in practice and to infuse life into it. In early June, Defense Minister Yazov told visitors privately that since the founding of the Presidential Council in late March, that body had met twice, but the Defense Council had not met at all.[14] At the 28th Party Congress in early July, Zaykov, after presenting a highly laudatory account of Gorbachev's organization of the national security decisionmaking bodies since 1985, made this extraordinary plea:

> I believe that *we must not destroy* the well-oiled mechanism for interdepartmental work on military-political issues. We *should use* its struc-

---

[12]Ironically, Zhivitsa—who at this stage was vigorously defending the central Soviet decisionmaking and control system—less than two years later, after the August 1991 coup, was to emerge as the Chief of the Ukrainian General Staff, intent on blocking all attempts to preserve the power of that system in Ukraine.

[13]*Kommunist Voorozhonykh Sil* (Communist of the Armed Forces), No. 11, June 1990, signed to press May 31, 1990, p. 27. Gorbachev had already stated in mid-March—when he was attempting to do away with the Defense Council—that only "a considerable proportion" of those who had been "involved in the work of the Defense Council" would "continue to take part" in helping the new executive president deal with defense matters. (*Pravda*, March 17, 1990.) Now that he felt obliged to revive the Defense Council as an institution, he still attempted to curtail military representation. In removing the service heads, Gorbachev resumed the accordion-like oscillation of Defense Council structure discussed earlier, and apparently returned to the restrictions on military participants seen under Brezhnev.

[14]Private communication. Yazov expressed the conviction that while the Presidential Council might eventually come to discuss broad issues of security policy like arms control, it was much too large and diversified a group to consider such issues as military hardware or force employment policy, which should remain the province of the Defense Council, which was a "narrower group."

tures in the Defense Council under the USSR president.[15] (Emphasis added.)

These polemical Zaykov statements suggested considerable ongoing uncertainty in the defense elite about Gorbachev's intentions, despite his April statement. These doubts were no doubt fostered by Gorbachev's strangely equivocal handling of the constitutional amendments in March as well as by his failure to convene the new Defense Council up to the summer.

Eventually, in mid-August, these doubts were for the time being resolved, when Gorbachev addressed a gathering of participants in a military exercise in Odessa. He now assured this audience that relations between the political and military leaderships were "fine" and "businesslike." He asserted that "an overhauled Defense Council has been set up and attached to the Presidential Council and the President," and that it would consider "all issues affecting military activity and the construction of the Armed Forces." To this end, he said, this revamped Defense Council "attached to the President" would meet in September to examine the draft concepts the Ministry of Defense had prepared on military reform.[16]

Two weeks later, at the beginning of September, this promised meeting duly took place under Gorbachev's chairmanship. Moreover, for the first time in Soviet history, the holding of a Defense Council session was publicly reported in the press the next day, and its agenda and decisions described in general terms.[17] The purposes of introducing such publicity for a Defense Council session were probably several. One was presumably to demonstrate to doubters that Gorbachev did intend to use the new version of the Defense Council. Another was to formalize and relegitimize a body that Gorbachev had placed in question by removing reference to it from the Constitution. And a third was to highlight the central subject of this particular Defense Council meeting—its consideration of the concept of Soviet military reform worked out by the Ministry of Defense.[18]

---

[15]*Pravda*, July 4, 1990.

[16]Moscow television service, August 17, 1990 (FBIS-SOV, August 20, 1990, p. 49).

[17]*Pravda*, September 2, 1990. This reportage resembled the public accounts of party Politburo meetings that Gorbachev had initiated some years earlier.

[18]The account of the meeting stated that the Council had heard reports on this subject not only from Minister Yazov but also from the service commanders, who were apparently invited as *ad hoc* participants on this occasion because of the nature of the topic, which included the question of "improving the structure of the services."

Subsequently, the revival of use of the Defense Council apparently proceeded in tandem with Gorbachev's retreat before military pressure in the fall and winter of 1990. In November 1990, Gorbachev assured a gathering of hostile military legislators that all defense questions were now being tackled "more vigorously" by the Defense Council"—a phrase conveying his acknowledgment that there had been a certain lack of vigor in defense decisionmaking earlier in the year.[19] In December, when Gorbachev proposed to the Congress of People's Deputies fresh constitutional amendments to abolish the Presidential Council and substitute a Security Council under himself, he alluded to the Defense Council as "one of the structural links in the Security Council."[20]

Even now, Gorbachev did not propose that the Defense Council be dignified by embodiment in the Constitution along with the new Security Council. Nevertheless, from the fall of 1990 on, there were further public references to the continued functioning of the Defense Council, including some allusions to specific meetings that had been held but not formally reported. In late November, Gorbachev referred to the Defense Council as the place where "the most fundamental questions [regarding arms negotiations] are examined and decisions made."[21] He also revealed that the future of the Soviet scientific potential for military research and development had been one of the topics recently discussed at a Defense Council meeting.[22]

Another such unannounced meeting apparently grappled with the sensitive political issue of whether nuclear testing should be resumed in Semipalatinsk, a notion bitterly opposed by Kazakhstan. In November 1990, B. A. Bukatov, Deputy Chairman of the Military Industrial Commission (VPK), asserted that "the issue of underground nuclear testing has recently been discussed at a session of the USSR President's Defense Council." He implied that he had participated (presumably as a special invitee to that session), but did not discuss decisions reached.[23]

---

[19] *Sovetskaya Rossiya*, November 15, 1990.

[20] *Pravda*, December 18, 1990.

[21] Moscow television, November 26, 1990 (FBIS-SOV, November 27, 1990, p. 39).

[22] *Ibid.*, p. 42.

[23] *Pravitelstvennyy Vestnik*, No. 47, November 1990. Bukatov said that in the wake of this session, a draft Supreme Soviet resolution on nuclear testing was being "worked on" with the participation of Russian and Kazakh representatives. He added that after the resolution was approved, the Council of Ministers would report on it to the Supreme Soviet. In the aftermath, however, no such resolution emerged.

In the aftermath of this Defense Council session, the question of resuming tests at Semipalatinsk proved to be a watershed issue, because it demonstrated that the Defense Council, even in this period of military ascendancy in Moscow, found itself unable to carry out a decision of great importance to the military. In December 1990, Marshal Yazov publicly claimed a need and right to resume testing in Semipalatinsk, because "there is nowhere else to test certain kinds of weapons."[24] Meanwhile, however, in Kazakhstan, local officials threatened Gorbachev with a "protest strike" if nuclear weapons tests were resumed in Semipalatinsk, "as follows from reports from the country's Defense Council."[25] Subsequently, a Kazakh parliamentary spokesman "denied media reports that nuclear arms tests will resume at the Semipalatinsk test site," asserting that "the reply of the Soviet Defense Council to their inquiry unequivocally states there have been no decisions on the continuation of tests in Semipalatinsk."[26] In July, Kazakh President Nazarbayev reiterated his insistence that the decision be left to a referendum of local inhabitants.[27]

In sum, for the better part of a year before the August 1991 attempted coup, the Semipalatinsk testing issue gradually became a cause of growing tension between Gorbachev, Yazov, and the Kazakh leadership. As this three-cornered contest went on, the Defense Council was paralyzed by the impasse.[28]

Meanwhile, during the last year of its existence the Defense Council was also increasingly involved in negotiations on other defense issues growing out of center-periphery relations. For example, in January 1991, the Estonian Supreme Soviet and the USSR Defense Council

---

[24]*Sovetskaya Rossiya*, December 21, 1990.

[25]*Komsomoskaya Pravda*, December 14, 1990.

[26]Moscow radio, December 27, 1990 (FBIS-SOV, December 28, 1990, p. 62). This statement suggested that someone had been conducting official correspondence with Kazakhstan in the name of the Defense Council, a body that had traditionally had no secretariat of its own to perform such functions between sessions. Presumably, the assurances in question were dictated by Gorbachev, but were sent in the name of the Council either by the General Staff (the traditional Defense Council secretariat) or by Gorbachev's presidential apparatus.

[27]*Komsomolskaya Pravda*, July 9, 1991. This account contained Kazakhstan's vigorous denial of a report three days earlier that Nazabayev had accepted a Gorbachev compromise offer to hold two further nuclear tests at Semipalatinsk in 1981 and then to end such tests. Originally, the Defense Council was said to have decided to end nuclear tests at Semipalatinsk only in January 1993, but retreated from this decision under Kazakh pressure. (*Komsomolskaya Pravda*, July 6, 1991.)

[28]In the wake of the failed August coup, Nazarbayev was to declare use of the Semipalatinsk test facilities permanently ended, and the new Soviet military leadership then tamely agreed.

were said to have "finally reached a compromise ... on the question of drafting young men for military service." The description of this agreement—like similar agreements on the deployment of draftees reached between Moscow and various other republics in the first half of 1991—suggested that the matter had been under negotiation for some time by the Ministry of Defense, and that the agreement had merely been ratified by Gorbachev and the Defense Council.[29]

In June 1991, a meeting of the Defense Council was for a second and last time formally reported in the press. Chaired by Gorbachev, this session was said to have examined "several issues of defense organization," including execution of the military reform, force maintenance, the troop withdrawal from Eastern Europe, and military housing. This communique also used language that served to highlight Gorbachev's authority over the Defense Council, noting that Gorbachev as president had given the "ministries and departments appropriate instructions on the matters discussed."[30]

THE SECURITY COUNCIL

In late 1990, the position of the temporarily reborn Defense Council was further complicated by Gorbachev's decision to replace the Presidential Council with a more selective body made up largely of ministers, to be called the Security Council. Although Gorbachev spoke of this Security Council as being concerned with security affairs in the broadest sense,[31] and although two foreign affairs specialists (Foreign Minister Bessmertnykh and presidential adviser Primakov) were among the nine men initially included, it soon became apparent that the main purpose intended for the new body was overwhelmingly internal, not external: that is, the interdepartmental coordination of policies affecting domestic security.

The Security Council's creation occurred in the midst of Gorbachev's move to the right in late 1990, and coincided with his temporary surrender to the pressure of the military-industrial complex for draconian measures to attempt to preserve the union. The emergence of this new organ was thus prompted by the ongoing disintegration of

---

[29]*Komsomolskaya Pravda*, January 17, 1991.

[30]TASS, June 27, 1991.

[31]Gorbachev address to Supreme Soviet, Moscow radio, March 7, 1991 (FBIS-SOV, March 8, 1991, p. 43). The constitutional provisions setting up the Security Council also said that it would be called on to draft recommendations to implement all-union policy for the country's defense. (TASS, March 7, 1991 (FBIS-SOV, March 7, 1991, p. 32).)

the union and by Gorbachev's wish to invent a mechanism that would give him more direct personal control of the interwoven political, economic, and coercive measures that were to be used to deal with the crisis. Consequently, foreign policy—and certainly defense policy—were from the outset peripheral concerns of the Security Council, although not entirely outside its purview.[32]

Thus, although some observers in Moscow and abroad compared the new Soviet Security Council to the U.S. National Security Council, its *raison d'etre* was almost the obverse of the American body, whose primary focus is external, not internal. Moreover, Gorbachev was apparently reluctant to build up a staff apparatus for the Security Council remotely comparable to that which the U.S. National Security Council possesses, and that helps make it a useful presidential tool for controlling and coordinating government departments. And finally, the exclusion of most defense and external security matters from the field of view of the Security Council meant that any staff it did obtain could in any case not be used to replace the General Staff as the secretariat of the Defense Council.

In short, Gorbachev had now adopted only half of the earlier-cited Velikhov February 1990 proposal for a Security and Defense Council. He had accepted the internal security half, the portion that had the least relevance to the U.S. institution Velikhov had cited as his model. Consequently, during the seven months that it remained in existence this new Soviet institution could neither replace the Defense Council nor threaten the General Staff's role there. Clearly, it was not intended to do anything of the kind.

THE NEW PRESIDENTIAL APPARAT, BOLDIN, AND BAKLANOV

Meanwhile, from late 1990 on, a significant apparat concerned with defense and security affairs had at last begun to emerge in the office of the presidency itself. It will be recalled that in Andropov's time, the installation of a sizable body of authoritative and fully cleared military expertise in the office of the top leader—then, the party General Secretary—had been proposed as a prerequisite to replacing the General Staff as the secretariat of the Defense Council. In princi-

---

[32]At a press conference in June 1991, Supreme Soviet Chairman Anatoliy Lukyanov is reported to have said that while the Defense Council deals with the army and defense industry, the Security Council oversees such matters as economic policy, foreign policy, and ecological security. (Radio Rossii, June 3, 1991, reported in RFE/RL (Radio Free Europe/Radio Liberty) Daily Report, No. 107, June 7, 1991.)

ple, the fact that such an extensive national security apparatus attached directly to the leader was now at last being put in place, for the first time in the post-Stalin era, could have raised a threat to the General Staff's role and to its influence over the Defense Council. In practice, however, this did not happen, because during the period leading up to the August events Gorbachev allowed his new presidential apparat to be staffed through transfers from the party Central Committee apparat, where many of the officials involved shared the perspective of the most reactionary and recalcitrant members of the General Staff. Indeed, two transferees from the party apparat who played key roles in this presidential staffing process were later to play central roles also in the attempted coup against Gorbachev. One was Valeriy Boldin, and the other was Oleg Baklanov.

Boldin was a close Gorbachev personal associate for more than a decade, whom Gorbachev, upon becoming General Secretary, had made head of the General Department of the Central Committee—in effect, head of the Politburo's administrative secretariat. Early in 1990, as soon as Gorbachev became the executive president, Boldin was concurrently appointed chief of the presidential staff; a year later, Gorbachev unsuccessfully sought to appoint Boldin to the Security Council as well.[33] Boldin was therefore widely regarded—both in Moscow and in the West—as a man who was permanently "in Gorbachev's pocket." Indeed, this misconception was apparently shared by Gorbachev.

In fact, Boldin, like Marshal Yazov, and like certain other former close associates of Gorbachev,[34] was a man whose loyalty to Gorbachev was being rapidly eroded by events. Boldin's ideological sympathies were apparently strongly aligned with diehard colleagues from the Central Committee apparat, and particularly with Baklanov, a personal friend who had been the Central Committee secretary for military industry during the years that Boldin was in charge of the Central Committee General Department.

---

[33]This nomination was rejected by the Soviet legislature, in part because many—remembering Brezhnev's promotion of his aide Chernenko—felt it unseemly to appoint to the Security Council a man considered only a personal Gorbachev flunky.

[34]Another striking example was Anatoliy Lukyanov, like Boldin a veteran of the Central Committee apparatus and a close Gorbachev lieutenant whom Gorbachev had installed as Chairman of the Supreme Soviet when Gorbachev was himself obliged to relinquish that post upon becoming executive president in the spring of 1990. Within a year, Lukyanov had begun to drift away from political support of Gorbachev and toward the right-wing alliance, and in August 1991 he was deeply implicated in the conspiracy to remove Gorbachev.

By late 1990, when Gorbachev began to build up the staff organization attached to the presidential office in place of the old apparat of the central party machine, the president apparently found it natural to use for this purpose personnel from the departments of the Central Committee that were simultaneously being eliminated. Boldin, the head of his staff and his trusted personal factotum,[35] was evidently given a great deal of responsibility in selecting individuals for such transfers and in setting up departments within the presidential staff.[36]

One such unit established in Gorbachev's staff in late 1990 has been variously described as a "department for military questions"[37] or the "President's defense and state security section."[38] This presidential department was staffed largely by recruits transferred from the Military Department of the Central Committee long supervised by party secretary Baklanov, and Baklanov was duly named to head the new staff department.[39]

These transferees from the Central Committee apparat to the presidential staff, in turn, evidently continued as before to influence the selection process for senior posts in the armed forces, ensuring the continued domination of like-minded conservatives there.[40] Indeed, Boldin, Baklanov, and many of those they brought to the presidential apparat apparently exercised considerable conservative influence of a more general nature on Gorbachev, preying on his fears of the left in late 1990 and helping to move him into his temporary alliance with the right and with the military-industrial complex.

Against this background, it is plausible to suppose, as some Russians have suggested, that Boldin played an important role in securing from Gorbachev the extraordinary preferment given the most impor-

---

[35]Boldin is quoted as having asserted privately: "Formally I'm considered head of the apparat . . . but my functions are perhaps wider, since I've been with Mikhail Sergeyevich from the first day he became General Secretary." (*Moscow News*, No. 37, September 1991.)

[36]One writer asserts that "once inside the Presidential office Boldin shuffled personnel in a big way." He was said to have been "one of the main pumps that kept the flow moving" from the Central Committee apparatus to the presidency, building the new apparat "using 'tested' people . . . from CPSU headquarters." (*Ibid.*)

[37]Speech by V. S. Smirnov to USSR Congress of People's Deputies, *Izvestiya*, September 4, 1991.

[38]Statement by Viktor Surikov in Gottemoeller and Aldrin.

[39]*Ibid.*

[40]Speech by V.S. Smirnov, *Izvestiya*, September 4, 1991.

tant alumnus of the military-industrial sector of the party apparat.[41] This was Boldin's friend Baklanov, whom Gorbachev in April 1991 appointed First Deputy Chairman of the revived Defense Council—in effect, the day-to-day manager of the council.

Gorbachev by this time had allowed an impressive combination of key national security decisionmaking functions to become concentrated in Baklanov's hands. Although the old Defense Department of the Central Committee had been abolished, it had in effect been reconstituted within the presidential staff, under Baklanov's direction. At the same time, even in the remnant of the old Central Committee machine, an advisory Defense Commission continued to exist, still chaired by Baklanov. Meanwhile, as the new First Deputy Chairman of the Defense Council, Baklanov now had control of the machinery of that body. And finally, Baklanov was apparently now a member of both (a) the arms control decisionmaking body (formerly known as the Politburo's Political Commission, now the President's Group on Negotiations) and also (b) the working group under that body that prepared recommendations for it. Indeed, in his capacity as head of the defense department of the president's staff, Baklanov also had the main responsibility for coordinating the views of the various defense agencies that supported the arms control working group.[42]

Baklanov's predecessor in both the Central Committee job and the Defense Council post, Lev Zaykov, apparently continued to work behind the scenes in the bureaucracy even after leaving the Politburo in the summer of 1990, and Zaykov is said to have continued to chair the President's Group on Negotiations through the summer of 1991.[43] Nevertheless, given Baklanov's accumulation of functions, he had evidently eclipsed Zaykov in importance well before he replaced Zaykov as the Defense Council first deputy in April 1991. This change in leading personalities mirrored the more aggressive political posture now assumed by the military-industrial complex. Zaykov had also been a conservative supporter of that complex, but his behavior had been conditioned somewhat by the fact that he had had much wider experience as a politician than had Baklanov. In the fall of 1989, when Gorbachev had named Zaykov First Deputy Chairman of the Defense Council, Zaykov had publicly asserted that this was done to ensure an "extra-departmental approach" when cutting the armed

---

[41]*Moscow News*, No. 37, September 1991.
[42]Gottemoeller and Aldrin.
[43]*Ibid.*

forces, a remark that was not very flattering to the Ministry of Defense.[44]

Zaykov's successor, Baklanov, was always more openly pugnacious in defending the military perspective. In the summer of 1990, while still a Central Committee secretary, he had publicly sneered at the "dangerous" propensity of "some of our diplomats"—that is, Shevardnadze—"to reach agreement with the other side at any price."[45] And a year later, after receiving his Defense Council appointment, Baklanov participated in a published roundtable discussion in which he shared the views expressed by three of the leading reactionaries of the military-industrial complex.[46]

In sum, so long as Baklanov remained in place as the Pooh Bah of national security decisionmaking, and so long as he and Boldin could ensure that like-minded apparatchiks would continue to be picked to provide staff support for Gorbachev in the presidential office, the conservative perspective of the military-industrial establishment could be reinforced on all the key fronts—ensuring continued conservative control of the commanding heights in the Defense Council, the Defense Ministry, the General Staff, the VPK, and the "military department" of the presidency. There was, as one opponent put it, a "pyramid of like-minded people from top to bottom."[47] When, during 1991, centrifugal Soviet trends nevertheless began to undermine this pyramid, and when Gorbachev began to turn away from his alliance with the military-industrial complex, many of its key figures were to turn against him. Prominent among them were Baklanov and Boldin.

THE MOMENTOUS CONSEQUENCES OF THE CENTRIFUGAL PROCESS

As it turned out, in 1991 the ongoing centrifugal process outside Moscow was to prove vastly more important for the future of the

---

[44]Moscow radio, November 22, 1989.

[45]Baklanov speech to 28th Party Congress, *Pravda*, July 7, 1990. In a transparent effort to drive a wedge between Shevardnadze and Gorbachev, Baklanov contrasted this "dangerous" tendency of "some diplomats" with the "well-considered standpoint" of the party General Secretary.

[46]*Den'* (Moscow), No. 9, May 1991. The published account of this roundtable discussion received a good deal of notoriety. The three men who took part with Baklanov were Col. Gen. I. N. Romanov, Admiral Chernavin, and *Den'* editor Aleksandr Prokhanov. Ominously, in view of what was to follow, this symposium openly discussed the possibility of a military takeover and the consequences that might ensue.

[47]Speech by V. S. Smirnov to USSR Congress of People's Deputies, *Izvestiya*, September 4, 1991.

Defense Council—and for the Soviet military institution as a whole—than were all Gorbachev's reorganizations and appointments in the capital.

During the months leading up to the August 1991 coup, the General Staff, the Military-Industrial Commission, and the other members of the defense complex discovered that this centrifugal process was steadily eroding their traditional ability to use the Defense Council to make and carry out unilateral decisions affecting the republics. Thus, as we have seen, the council found itself more and more obliged to bargain rather than to command, seeking unpalatable and unprecedented compromises—with, for example, Kazakhstan regarding nuclear testing and with Estonia and other republics regarding conscription. Despite Gorbachev's temporary surrender to the right-wing alliance in the winter of 1990, the Defense Council and the Defense Ministry remained unable to compel the republics to fulfill conscription quotas. The ongoing decline in the overall rate of compliance with the semiannual call-up did not abate in the spring of 1991, and average unit readiness levels continued to fall. Thus, the continuing struggle within the Defense Ministry and the Defense Council over the nature and pace of military reform and the scope of planned force reduction was increasingly overshadowed by a growing reality beyond the decisionmaking framework: the unplanned shrinking of the armed forces as a result of the center's steadily diminishing ability to enforce conscription.

Equally important, as the power of the purse gravitated away from the center, the military hardware program decisions and the overall military spending levels traditionally worked out and approved by the Defense Council now became increasingly vulnerable to pressure from the republics. The privileged position of military industry was already being eroded by the overall economic environment—the decline in orders for some weapons categories, the disruption of some supply channels, the reduction of the subsidies that had preserved privileged wage rates, and the new competition from high-paying cooperatives for skilled labor. The centrifugal process immensely aggravated these trends. As 1991 went on, the republic leaders began to use the financial leverage they had seized—the new power to withhold money from the center—to press for further radical reductions in the central military budget.

As the shortfalls in revenue received from the republics grew, Gorbachev's central government was increasingly obliged to rely upon the printing press to create the funds demanded by its budgetary priorities, which still included preservation of a huge mass army and a concomitant weapons stock. But the uncontrolled printing of rubles, in turn, fed a runaway inflation that rapidly undermined the value of the defense allocations approved in the Defense Council and pushed through the legislature. The Defense Ministry sought to protect itself by demanding a heightened defense budget allocation indexed against inflation, but this expedient also proved inadequate as the printing of rubles and inflation accelerated.

All these pressures on the center's ability to enforce priorities multiplied after two landmark political events that greatly strengthened the centrifugal forces contending with the center. The first was Gorbachev's April 1991 meeting at Novo-Ogarevo with Boris Yeltsin and eight other republic leaders in which Gorbachev turned away from his short-lived alliance with the forces of the right in order to seek an understanding that might make possible agreement on a new union treaty. This step in effect conceded and legitimized a shift in the balance of power away from the center, and thus also away from the leaders of the military-industrial complex whose interests were greatly dependent on the old centralized structure.

The second landmark event was Yeltsin's election as president of the Russian Federation by popular vote in June 1991, which pushed further the ongoing shift in the political balance. Among other things, this election demonstrated Yeltsin's ability to win widespread voting support from the troops, and it also dramatized his increasingly visible alliance with a reformist wing of the military leadership opposed to the views of those still in control of the General Staff and the Defense Council.

Meanwhile, as the struggle over the new union treaty evolved, the leaders of Russia and Ukraine began to demand an unprecedented share of control over military industrial plants on their territory. By the summer of 1991, on the eve of the attempted coup, the republics had begun to take organizational measures to attempt to force from the center an explicit transfer of authority in military-industrial matters. A version of the draft union treaty published in late June called for republic participation in "defining the military policy of the Union" and "national security strategy" and in "resolving questions connected with troop activities and the locating of military facilities on republic territories" and "directing defense-complex enterprises."[48]

---

[48]*Krasnaya Zvezda*, June 28, 1991. See Stephen Foye, "Gorbachev's Return to Reform: What Does It Mean for the Armed Forces?" *RFE/RL Report on the USSR*, Vol. 3, No. 28, July 12, 1991, pp. 5–9.

While these formulations remained ambiguous, the republics now took the offensive to spell them out.

In mid-July 1991, Yeltsin's chief military representative, Col. Gen. Konstantin Kobets,[49] organized a meeting in Kiev with military representatives of Ukraine, Kazakhstan, and Belarus to draw up an additional protocol to be added to the new draft union treaty that would formalize and make concrete a reallocation of authority on defense and military industry.[50] They apparently insisted that the new union treaty explicitly confirm the republics' right to control military enterprises located on their territory, a right that was now publicly claimed by Ukraine.[51]

These claims were anathema to the leaders of the VPK and to men such as Baklanov, who were already fighting a losing battle to slow the rapid erosion of central ability to allocate resources to military industry, and who believed acceptance of the proposed treaty protocol would mean decisive defeat in this struggle. These men believed that if the treaty formally abrogated their traditional central monopoly of control over the defense industry through the VPK and the Defense Council, they would have lost for good their fight to preserve the privileged position of military industry in the allocation of Soviet economic resources.

In addition, the republics in the summer of 1991 simultaneously began to press more and more insistently for admission of their

---

[49]Kobets, a seemingly orthodox former General Staff officer whose transfer Yeltsin had negotiated with Moiseyev, now revealed himself with increasing frankness as opposed to Moiseyev's perspective. In a July interview, Kobets was quoted as saying that "the republics no longer want to remain passive spectators of the destruction of their wealth, which, instead of serving to create an efficient army . . . is still being used to develop too big a defense system which is impotent and crippled by overlapping structures." (*Le Monde*, July 17, 1991.) During the crisis over the August attempted coup, Kobets was temporarily proclaimed Defense Minister for the Russian Republic, and led Yeltsin's military defense against the forces deployed by the KGB [Committee for State Security] and General Staff.

[50]The draft protocol was said to have expanded the joint sphere of competence of the union and the republics to such issues as determining the level of "adequate defense" and the defense budget. (*Ibid.*; see also the account of the meeting issued by Yeltsin's "Russian Information Agency" (Radio "Mayak" (Moscow), July 18, 1991).) The Kiev meeting was attended by two representatives of the General Staff appointed by Moiseyev. (*Nezavisimaya Gazeta*, August 1, 1991 (FBIS-SOV, August 14, 1991, p. 50).) The central military leadership made it clear, however, that it had not reached agreement with the republic representatives. (*Krasnaya Zvezda*, July 20, 1991.) After the attempted coup, one Russian parliamentary official claimed that some in the General Staff had been willing to reach a compromise agreement, but that the Defense Ministry—that is, Yazov—had refused. (Sergey Stepashin interview, Radio Moscow, September 2, 1991 (FBIS-SOV, September 4, 1991, pp. 68–69).)

[51]*Nezavisimaya Gazeta*, August 1, 1991.

representatives to the USSR Defense Council itself. In the fall of 1990, this notion had surfaced for the first time during early discussions about a new union treaty,[52] and early in 1991, it had been publicly endorsed by another Yeltsin defense adviser, Col. Gen. Dmitriy Volkogonov.[53] Soon thereafter, the Russian parliament had adopted a resolution formally demanding the inclusion of republic leaders in the USSR Defense Council.[54] Now, at the mid-July meeting in Kiev, the representatives of the republics are said to have discussed the creation of a new Defense Council that would include both republic and central leaders and would carry out a fundamental reorganization of the existing defense decisionmaking structure. The republics are also said to have demanded that in this new structure, their leaders should have an "absolute veto" over all decisions.[55]

Most ominous of all for men such as Yazov and Baklanov was the perception that Gorbachev was now leaning increasingly toward accommodation of these demands. Later, after the attempted coup had failed, Gorbachev asserted that he had said "forthrightly to a narrow circle" that he was preparing a "reorganization of the whole state structure"—including the army, the KGB, and the Ministry of Internal Affairs—to take effect after "the signing of a union treaty and the departure of some republics."[56] Although Gorbachev after the coup had some incentive to exaggerate what he had been intending to do, there had been hints beforehand that he had indeed been planning organizational steps unwelcome to the military leadership. In late June he had defended his policy of concessions to the West against recent public attacks by Yazov and Kryuchkov, and alluded to the economy as "overmilitarized."[57] A few days later he told a military audience that "the defense complex is obliged to adapt itself,"

---

[52]This notion was presented by Igor Novoselov, a consultant for the USSR Supreme Soviet secretariat, who stated that each republic should have a representative with a deciding vote on the Defense Council, and that republics should have the right to participate in deciding such issues as the number of conscripts and strength of the armed forces and the military budget. (*Argumenty i fakty*, No. 40, 1990.)

[53]Interview in *Soyuz* (Moscow), No. 6, February 1991, in FBIS-SOV, May 30, 1991, p. 48.

[54]TASS, February 1, 1991.

[55]Radio Mayak (Moscow), July 18, 1991, cited by RFE/RL Daily Report, No. 136, July 19, 1991, carried on Sovset computer network.

[56]Interview on Central Television, October 12, 1991 (FBIS-SOV, October 15, 1991, p. 30).

[57]USSR Supreme Soviet question and answer session, Moscow Central Television, June 21, 1991 (FBIS-SOV, June 24, 1991, p. 39). Unlike his behavior the previous fall, Gorbachev now took the occasion to defend Shevardnadze as well.

that "it is necessary to bring arms production into line with . . . doctrine," and that "profound military reform cannot be avoided."[58]

And most important, Gorbachev took an overt step that strongly implied that he intended to acquiesce in the demand of republic leaderships for representation on the Defense Council. In February, when the Russian Supreme Soviet had passed a resolution demanding Yeltsin's admission to the Defense Council, it had also urged Gorbachev to include the chairmen of local soviets as members of regional military councils.[59] In late June, Gorbachev indeed issued a decree redefining the status of the military councils to exclude local party leaders and to permit, instead, inclusion of the local soviet leaders.[60] The leaders of the General Staff and the Military-Industrial Commission almost certainly interpreted this step as presaging an analogous move at the central level, and feared that the new structure of the Defense Council demanded by the republics would be imposed on them as a result of the signing of the new union treaty.

THE PRESSURES AND INDUCEMENTS TO ATTEMPT A COUP

In sum, the growing pressures for drastic institutional change contributed significantly to the decision of those thus threatened to launch the August 1991 coup. Although there were various motives shared to differing degrees by the coup participants, a prominent motive was certainly the hope to halt the centrifugal process by preventing the imminent signing of a union treaty that would formalize a vast further reduction of the influence over the national security decisionmaking process still enjoyed by the military-industrial alliance.

At the same time, Gorbachev had done little in the summer of 1991 to reduce the capability for desperate action by those whom he had placed in positions of power and whose power was most threatened by the new trends. Evidently because he feared the consequences of any overt step against them, he did not attempt to punish generals who signed threatening public statements, he did not remove KGB Chairman Kruychkov or Minister of the Interior Pugo despite their open defiance of him in the legislature, and he did not depose his Defense Council deputy Baklanov even after Baklanov toyed in print

---

[58]Speech to military graduates, Radio Mayak, June 26, 1991 (FBIS-SOV, June 26, 1991, p. 56).

[59]TASS, February 1, 1991.

[60]TASS, June 24, 1991.

with the notion of a military takeover.[61] And finally, apparently unaware of Boldin's sentiments, he did not remove Boldin as his closest personal aide.

An extraordinary combination of circumstances thus moved the coup participants to act. The economic disaster and the centrifugal process were together rapidly whittling away at their power, and they had reason to believe that the results of this process would soon be constitutionally confirmed with Gorbachev's approval. On the other hand, they could have gotten the impression from Gorbachev's past behavior and from his visible inhibitions in dealing with them that he might possibly again be bullied into switching sides.[62]

Thus, although the participants were surely aware that an unconstitutional move against the president might precipitate a dangerous split in the armed forces,[63] they could nevertheless hope, given Gorbachev's long record of vacillation and political oscillation, that once they had seized power he might be browbeaten into providing a constitutional cover for what they had done. This did not happen. In the meantime, their anxiety to secure a constitutional facade for their actions inhibited them from taking decisive and bloody steps in sufficient time to preempt resistance, and thus guaranteed that when Gorbachev failed to provide his blessings, the coup would be likely to collapse.

---

[61] *Den'* (Moscow), No. 9, May 1991.

[62] Afterward, during the investigation of the coup, the Russian deputy chief prosecutor stated that although Gorbachev had given "no hint" to the conspirators to encourage them to act, "however, his long relations with members of the conspiracy, who were his closest associates, and some special features of his character gave them ... the right to think that sooner or later, after one, two, three days, they would be able to draw him to their side." (*New York Times*, January 22, 1992.)

[63] Of the three most important participants in the coup—First Deputy Defense Council Chairman Baklanov, KGB Chairman Kryuchkov, and Defense Minister Yazov—Yazov was probably the most intimately sensitive to the danger that the coup might divide the army. Yazov was therefore the most lukewarm and reluctant of the plotters to accept the consequences of a widespread use of violence. The underlying differences within the junta on this central issue contributed greatly to the coup's failure.

7. THE END OF THE SOVIET STATE AND THE FUTURE OF DEFENSE DECISIONMAKING

THE FIRST INSTITUTIONAL RESULTS OF THE FAILED COUP

In the wake of the failure of the August 1991 coup, Gorbachev's decisionmaking institutional arrangements for national security were necessarily thrown into disarray and discredited. A majority of Gorbachev's Security Council and, as Yeltsin pointed out, the core of his Defense Council[1] had supported the putsch. Consequently, not only these men but the two institutions they had dominated seemed to be delegitimized.[2] There were, in fact, public demands that the Defense Council be legally abolished "to guarantee that another coup does not take place."[3] And although apparently no such formal step was taken, this institution does seem to have temporarily vanished into limbo after the coup, since so many of its leading figures were now in prison.

The issue of what institutions were to be created to replace the old ones now hinged on the outcome of the two-front political struggle that followed. On the one hand, the new contest over decisionmaking authority involved the rising and fading forces in Moscow—Yeltsin's Russia and Gorbachev's mortally weakened all-union regime. On the other hand, there now simultaneously arose another, new and growing struggle—which soon became all-important—between Yeltsin's Russian leadership in Moscow and the leaders of certain other republics.

In the aftermath of the putsch attempt, repeated efforts were made to create new interrepublic defense coordination mechanisms that would

---

[1]On August 20, during the coup period, Yeltsin's "Decree No. 64" asserted that "the Vice President of the USSR, the Minister of Defense of the USSR, the First Deputy Chairman of the Defense Council of the USSR, and other members of the Defense Council have embarked upon a criminal path. . . ." (Moscow Radio Triana, August 20, 1991 (FBIS-SOV, August 21, 1991, p. 57).)

[2]A week after the coup's collapse, speakers on a Moscow television panel denounced the old Defense Council as "an element of a totalitarian state and a totalitarian system," and said its existence had "represented a threat to the country's security" because it had been "one of the temptations of these conspirators who counted on the entire military organization being constrained under a single leadership." (Moscow central television, August 31, 1991 (FBIS-SOV, September 10, 1991, p. 55).)

[3]Yuriy Ryzhov statement at session of USSR Supreme Soviet, August 26, 1991 (FBIS-SOV, August 29, 1991, p. 35).

somehow reconcile the incompatible demands of centralized control and real republic sovereignty. In September, the Defense Ministry under its new leadership was reported to be circulating a three-page document that alluded to the need to preserve a central command system while giving republics a much greater say in military policy.[4] Seemingly endless debates on how to do this continued in the fall, as interim decisionmaking arrangements in Moscow were adjusted in *ad hoc* fashion to reflect the drastic change in the balance of political power.

In principle, ultimate authority over security affairs—like authority over all other broad policy issues—was now transferred, for the time being, to a new State Council composed of Gorbachev and the republic leaders.[5] In practice, however, the most sensitive security-related decisions were apparently decided, also for the time being, privately and informally between Yeltsin and Gorbachev. Although Gorbachev retained the titular power of appointment, and the other republic leaders retained as a group the titular power of confirmation through the State Council, Yeltsin and the Russian government obtained dominant influence over the central military machinery in the immediate wake of the coup, and never relinquished it.

Thus, the early appointments of army Generals Yevgeniy Shaposhnikov and Vladimir Lobov as Defense Minister and Chief of the General Staff, respectively, were evidently made by Gorbachev upon Yeltsin's insistence, and subsequently formally confirmed by the State Council. Similarly, very early after the coup crisis, Yeltsin, but not the other republic leaders, appears to have obtained an equal share with Gorbachev in political (although not yet operational) control over the release of Soviet nuclear weapons.[6]

---

[4]*Wall Street Journal*, September 13, 1991.

[5]The State Council, wrote a *Pravda* observer on October 18th, "is vested with full authority in . . . military building and the elaboration and implementation of defense policy." Minister of Defense Shaposhnikov thus referred, for example, in September to "new documents recently adopted by the USSR State Council upon our presentation" to deal with military pay and housing. (*Argumenty i Fakty*, No. 38, September 1991.) And in early November, when the State Council responded to pressure from Yeltsin to abolish some 80 all-union ministries, it also "examined the fate of the Union Ministry of Defense behind closed doors with a few people present," and agreed to preserve this ministry for the time being. (Radio Rossii, November 5, 1991 (FBIS-SOV, November 5, 1991, p. 21).) During the four months that it existed, the State Council appears to have served in defense matters as an arena in which the struggle among the republics evolved, rendering the joint decisions it adopted less and less relevant to the underlying political realities.

[6]Statement by Russian Vice President Aleksandr Rutskoy in interview by *Die Welt* (Bonn), October 14, 1991. In December, Yeltsin's senior military adviser General Kobets asserted that "since the August putsch attempt," Yeltsin had been accompanied

THE LAST APPEARANCE OF THE USSR DEFENSE COUNCIL

Within six weeks, the informal arrangements were found insufficient. By the beginning of October, despite the opprobrium the coup plotters had brought to the Defense Council, Yeltsin and Gorbachev temporarily found themselves in agreement to revive this institution, for a pressing reason. At this point, they were suddenly obliged to react to President Bush's late September announcement of U.S. unilateral nuclear disarmament measures and strategic proposals. Some top-level joint body more restricted than the State Council was needed to consider expert testimony and recommendations (presumably, from the General Staff) and to make decisions on the unilateral measures the Soviet Union would adopt in response. (As noted earlier, the Defense Council in the Gorbachev era had been responsible for such unilateral initiatives, subject to approval by the Politburo up to 1990, and by the president thereafter.)

On October 1, almost immediately after receipt of the U.S. statement, a decree was issued by Gorbachev identifying the members of a new, truncated, six-man Defense Council. This revised and—as it was to prove—final version of the USSR Defense Council now included, in addition to Gorbachev as chairman, Russian President Yeltsin, Minister of Defense Shaposhnikov, Chief of the General Staff Lobov, Foreign Minister Boris Pankin, and Vadim Bakatin, Director of the Interrepublican Security Service (the successor organization at that point to the KGB).[7]

Yeltsin probably acquiesced for the time being in reviving this institution not only because it was needed to coordinate a reply to the United States, but also because publication of the new Defense Council membership tacitly confirmed the difference between his status as leader of Russia—and presumptive heir to the Soviet nuclear potential—and that of the other republic leaders, none of whom were

---

by "a man with a black bag"—presumably, communications gear. (*Le Monde*, December 16, 1991.) Yeltsin staff officials denied, however, that Yeltsin at this stage had control over any portion of the launch codes. (*Postfactum* (Moscow), November 19, 1991 (FBIS-SOV, November 20, 1991, p. 54).)

[7]*Vedomosti Verkhovnogo Soveta SSSR*, No. 41, cited by Victor Yasmann in RFE/RL Daily Report, No. 221, November 21, 1991. The publication of the membership of the Defense Council was unprecedented. Two days after the decree was issued, a Radio Moscow military observer said that on instructions from Gorbachev, "a special group has been set up in Moscow to respond to George Bush's nuclear disarmament initiative," and that "part of the group are Soviet military leaders." This was presumably an allusion to the new Defense Council. The observer confirmed that the Treaty and Legal Directorate of the General Staff was one of the organizations "scrutinizing the American proposals." (Radio Moscow, October 3, 1991 (FBIS-SOV, October 4, 1991, p. 36).)

included in the new Defense Council. However, before the decisions and proposals adopted were announced a week later as the Soviet response to the U.S. initiative, those aspects of the Soviet decisions that affected strategic nuclear weapons systems in Ukraine, Kazakhstan, and Belarus were apparently subjected to perfunctory coordination by the presidents of the republics concerned.[8]

Meanwhile, the October 1 Gorbachev decree reviving the Defense Council called for the drafting of Defense Council statutes by November 1.[9] This never happened, however, because the continued existence of this body was to be undermined by the further rapid deterioration of willingness by the republics to support such central institutions.

THE IMPACT OF FRAGMENTATION ON DEFENSE DECISIONMAKING

During the initial weeks after the failure of the coup, Yeltsin seemed to be testing the possibility of preserving a vestigial remnant of the Soviet state—including Gorbachev in a figurehead role—as an instrument for maintaining the Russian republic's ascendancy over the remnants of the Soviet empire. By mid-October at the latest, however, he had come to abandon this notion, for two reasons. One reason concerned his attitude toward Gorbachev and the other involved the behavior of the other republics.

First, despite Yeltsin's powerful new leverage over Gorbachev, he and many other Russian leaders found their anomalous relationship with the vestige of the center increasingly irksome. Gorbachev and his associates were even now by no means tame puppets; particularly in the economic sphere, they represented priorities and programs often quite different from Yeltsin's as well as institutional constraints upon his

---

[8]*New York Times*, October 9, 1991. A month later, when the USSR announced withdrawal of previous objections to an "Open Skies" treaty allowing verification overflights of the Soviet Union and the United States, the Soviet representative asserted that all the Soviet republics had endorsed this change. (*Washington Post*, November 6, 1991.) Such approval may have been obtained at the State Council meeting held on November 4, the day before the "Open Skies" announcement. Presumably, the change in the Soviet position had been discussed in detail and approved in the new Defense Council.

[9]Some military leaders were obviously hoping that the reborn Defense Council could be strengthened and used to consolidate the existence of unified forces. On the same day that Gorbachev signed the Defense Council decree, Chief of the General Staff Lobov wrote that "it would seem expedient for the Army to be led by a supreme commander in chief in the shape of the president, with an organ under him to which the Armed Forces and their institutions would be subordinate." (*Trud*, October 1, 1991.)

freedom of action. Gorbachev's continuing struggles to obtain a union treaty were now seen by Yeltsin as an effort to revive and perpetuate an autonomous central authority that would remain largely outside of the Russian government's policy control. Yeltsin also resented Gorbachev's continued use of his foreign policy role, with the encouragement of the West, as a means of propping up a facade of continued domestic preeminence.

Second, and probably more important, the increasing hostility shown by some republics toward preserving any form of central, all-union authority compelled Yeltsin in any case to move in the same direction. Although certain republics—notably Armenia, Kazakhstan, and the Central Asian states—wanted for their own reasons to keep a central authority in some guise,[10] others, and above all Ukraine, grew openly opposed to the notion. The inability of the republics to agree upon a formula for a new central economic coordinating mechanism made it apparent to the Russian leaders that Russia could carry out desperately needed economic reform only if it cut free from the institutional baggage of the Soviet state. Consequently, by mid-October Yeltsin was warning of his intention the next month to transfer Russian funding from most all-union institutions to their Russian counterparts. This unilateral Russian move to force the closing down of most of the all-union government was duly ratified by the State Council, was begun in November, and was completed in December.

But although Yeltsin almost certainly did not wish it, his decision to dismantle the central governmental apparatus inevitably also accelerated the slide toward formal division of the Soviet armed forces and fragmentation of the central military decisionmaking process. That process of military splintering was lamented not only by the professional military leaders in Moscow, but also by most Russian political leaders—naturally enough, since the central military machine that was being disrupted and fragmented was now seen by everyone, more and more nakedly, as Russia's machine. This perception grew rapidly after the November termination of most other central institutions of the old Soviet state.

Although Yeltsin then continued Russian funding of the Soviet Ministry of Defense, and thus for the time being maintained the pretense that this was an ongoing all-union institution independent of

---

[10]The Central Asian attitude was driven partly by the vain hope that a preserved Soviet state might continue to serve as a vehicle for tacit Russian subsidies to their region, and partly by the hope that a center led by Gorbachev could continue to serve as an institutional barrier against Russian nationalism.

Russia, few could believe this contention once the Ministry was left standing alone without a surrounding all-union government. In early November, the State Council at Shaposhnikov's urging tried to deal with this problem by finally creating a "Council of Ministers of Defense of Sovereign States" that would meet periodically to discuss "general matters relating to military policy."[11] But this long-delayed step was a lame expedient that could not change the trend in perceptions.

Ukraine's leaders had in any case already made it clear that they had no illusions about who would henceforth control the Moscow machinery of the Soviet army, and that they were unwilling to remain subject to that machinery. Although the attention of the outside world was necessarily drawn mainly to the danger of fragmentation of nuclear control, initially the immediate Ukranian concerns were the Soviet nonnuclear, general-purpose forces on Ukrainian soil which (unlike the nuclear missiles) were potential concrete instruments of political domination and therefore represented the most serious long-range threat to the viability of Ukrainian independence. In mid-October, the Ukrainian leaders therefore announced that they intended to create their own sizable[12] army from the Soviet general-purpose forces stationed in Ukraine. Equally important politically, they made it clear that no general-purpose ground forces not subordinated to Ukrainian authorities would be allowed to remain in Ukraine. A strong Ukrainian consensus soon emerged on this point, and was eventually reinforced by the results of the early December Ukrainian referendum on independence.

Ever since the failure of the August coup, Defense Minister Shaposhnikov and Chief of the General Staff Lobov had had ample warnings that Ukraine was unlikely to continue to accept centrally controlled nonnuclear forces on its soil. The Ukrainian leadership from the start had rejected the opening bargaining position of the military leaders in Moscow. Prefigured in earlier plans for military reform, the General Staff's proposal had been that each republic might set up a limited National Guard or Republic Guard of its own, composed of no more than a few thousand men, to be created by

---

[11] Shaposhnikov news conference reported by Moscow radio, November 5, 1991 (FBIS-SOV, November 5, 1991, p. 35). As early as August 28, such a council of republic ministers of defense had been publicly proposed to function as a "committee of the Defense Ministry" by Yeltsin's chief military adviser General Kobets. (Kobets interview on BBC television, August 28, 1991 (FBIS-SOV, September 3, 1991, p. 87).)

[12] A maximum size of some 420,000 men was publicly postulated for this army—a figure arbitrarily derived from the size of the Ukrainian population but not seriously intended as a force goal.

redesignating certain contingents of KGB and Interior Ministry troops already stationed on its territory. Along the same line, republics with coastlines might inherit a small coastal flotilla. In this scheme, the remaining bulk of forces of all types would remain under unified control from Moscow.

To lend verisimilitude to these notions, the Russian military and political leaderships fought off plans by radicals to create a sizable Russian army, and endorsed only the principle of a small Russian Guard. But although the Belorussian, Armenian, and Central Asian republics throughout the fall of 1991 were inclined to accept the General Staff blueprint for unified forces, the Moldovans, the Azeris—and above all, the Ukrainians—were not. The rapidly stiffening Ukrainian attitude was made clear to Shaposhnikov in a series of consultations in Kiev and Moscow between August and November. As time went on, the last Soviet Defense Minister began more and more to hint that if he could not obtain "unified" forces, he might eventually settle for "joint" ones—by which he implied that he meant republic armies or portions thereof earmarked and resubordinated in some fashion to a central leadership.[13]

THE NUCLEAR PROBLEM

Soviet nuclear forces meanwhile presented a problem of a different kind, particularly because in this realm outside pressures were more directly involved in Soviet organizational issues. The ongoing disintegration of the union evoked alarm in the West over the dangerous possibilities inherent in any weakening of central controls over nuclear weapons. The concern was particularly great with respect to the thousands of tactical nuclear weapons scattered throughout the Soviet Union, which Gorbachev had now agreed to destroy.

Since long before the coup attempt, the General Staff had begun the protracted process of withdrawing nuclear weapons—and particularly their warheads—from the periphery and concentrating them in the

---

[13]Most other non-Ukrainian military leaders took a similar position. Chief of the General Staff Lobov urged that the bulk of the forces be permanently controlled in unified fashion by some collegial military leadership in the center in which all republics would be represented. Failing that, he wished to have each republic designate forces to be operationally subordinate to a joint command in Moscow. (*Krasnaya Zvezda*, October 23, 1991.) Kobets envisaged beginning with united forces, and then at some later stage changing over to joint forces. (TASS, October 8, 1991 (FBIS-SOV, October 10, 1991, p. 4).)

three Slavic republics.[14] Now, as political fragmentation accelerated, so did Western pressure on the republics to permit a transfer of all such weapons to Russia for safe storage until destruction. These pressures were coupled with Western demands that whatever else happened to the Soviet state, unified control over all nuclear weapons must remain. There was and still is, however, an intrinsic tension between the overwhelming centrifugal process and this isolated element of centralization.

The problem was compounded by the increasing perception in the non-Russian republics that centralized control of nuclear weapons was tantamount to Russian control and would become an instrument of Russian political leverage. Statements by Russian leaders tended to confirm that impression. On September 4, Yeltsin told the Congress of People's Deputies that "We have to retain the armed forces under direct control of the center, and in particular, nuclear weapons. . . . Russia, in the first place, guarantees the unity of the nuclear potential of the army. . . . And special structures are being created for this."[15] On the same day, Yeltsin explained in a CNN interview that "we have set up a committee to control nuclear weapons," implying that this was the "special structure" in question. He then made it clear that Russia would play a unique role in this structure. In the same context, he claimed that strategic nuclear weapons in Ukraine were already "being pulled out" to Russia, and also that those in Kazakhstan "will be transferred to Russia."[16]

These statements proved inflammatory. Ten days later, Kazakh President Nazarbayev publicly reacted, saying he did not agree that Russia alone should have control of nuclear weapons, a position that he has maintained ever since. Nazarbayev opposed the suggestion that all the Soviet Union's nuclear weapons be moved to Russia, and demanded that the nuclear arsenal be placed under the control of a

---

[14] In December 1991, General Geliy Batenin, an adviser to the Russian Foreign Ministry, claimed privately that all tactical nuclear warheads had been removed from the Baltic states, Transcaucasia, and Central Asia, although delivery vehicles remained. (RFE/RL Daily Report, No. 236, December 13, 1991.) Earlier, the Western press had quoted "Soviet sources" as revealing that the General Staff was already withdrawing tactical nuclear weapons from Ukraine in order to "avoid problems of control in the near future," but was allegedly doing so "quietly, so as not to antagonize the Ukrainians." (*Washington Post*, October 24, 1991.) The very leak of this report was of course incompatible with withdrawing the weapons "quietly."

[15] *New York Times*, September 4, 1991.

[16] Yeltsin asserted that "apart from the central government, we want Russia to control nuclear weapons and to be responsible for nuclear weapons on the territory of Russia, and . . . we want to keep a finger on the button as well." (*New York Times*, September 4, 1991.)

special commission attached to the State Council.[17] Even in Ukraine, where antinuclear sentiment is particularly powerful because of the Chernobyl disaster, voices were now heard expressing reservations about the long-professed goal of a nuclear-free Ukraine, arguing that a Ukraine that did not retain some nuclear weapons would in the future be in a disadvantageous position alongside a nuclear-armed Russia.[18] Although this remained a minority view, more tenacious opposition now emerged to the notion of transferring tactical nuclear weapons and strategic warheads from Ukraine to Russia for storage and destruction. Finally, the Ukrainian leadership remained most reluctant of all to allow Yeltsin to exercise unilateral control over any nuclear weapons left on Ukrainian soil.

THE COMMONWEALTH

The December 1 Ukrainian referendum approving independence was the precipitating factor that compelled the contending leaderships to take steps to confront these differences, if not to finally resolve them. A few days later, Ukraine abrogated the old treaty by which it had adhered to the Soviet Union. With the old union (and its military control structure) effectively doomed in any case by the Ukrainian action, Yeltsin quickly moved to reach agreement with Ukraine and Belarus to put an end to the USSR and to create a "Commonwealth of Independent States." The Minsk declaration that initially embodied the commonwealth agreement pledged to "preserve and support common military and strategic space under a common command." But there was to be no full consensus on the meaning of this vague formula, as became clear when the republic leaders met twice more in December to try to spell it out.

On the nuclear side of the issue, a measure of understanding initially seemed to be reached two weeks after the Minsk gathering, when eight other republics met in Alma-Ata with the three Slavic states to adhere to their Commonwealth. By now Ukraine, under Western prodding, had acknowledged agreement to expedite the withdrawal of all tactical and strategic nuclear warheads and all strategic missiles deployed on Ukrainian territory for storage and eventual destruction

---

[17]TASS, September 15, 1991, quoting from Nazarbayev interview with *Tokyo Shimbun*, September 15, 1991.

[18]Indeed, even in Belarus (which was much less assertive in opposing Russia than was Ukraine, and where public opinion was at least equally hostile to nuclear weapons) the new local defense minister eventually expressed a similar longing to keep some nuclear weapons as an offset to Russia's. (Statement by Pyotr Chaus, TASS, December 11, 1991, cited in RFE/RL Daily Report, No. 235, December 12, 1991.)

in Russia.[19] At Alma-Ata, the four republics on whose territory strategic nuclear systems were present (Russia, Ukraine, Belarus, and Kazakhstan) signed an agreement confirming that the Russian president Yeltsin would in the meantime exercise sole supreme operational control of these weapons, subject to a political veto by the other three republic leaders.[20]

A week further on, at the very end of the year, this arrangement was reiterated in a Strategic Forces Agreement signed in Minsk by the Commonwealth members, which specified that the Russian president would decide about the use of nuclear weapons "in agreement with" Ukraine, Belarus, and Kazakhstan, and also "in consultation" with the other republics. This agreement also declared that all tactical nuclear weapons in Ukraine would be dismantled by July 1, 1992, and the strategic missiles by the end of 1994. In the meantime, Ukraine agreed that all nuclear weapons on its territory would remain under the control of the new Combined Strategic Forces Command, now headed by former USSR Defense Minister Shaposhnikov.[21]

However, even this nuclear understanding, cobbled together to assuage Western concerns about proliferation, retained certain important anomalies. Kazakhstan retained enduring reservations about allowing strategic nuclear weapons on its soil to be either disarmed or transferred to Russia while Russia remained a nuclear power. In addition, Ukraine's sweeping pledge in the agreement to subordinate all nuclear weapons in Ukraine to the Combined Strategic Forces Command was not literally accurate.

Two weeks after the agreement was signed the chief of staff of the Ukrainian armed forces, Maj. Gen. Georgiy Zhivitsa, told the Western press that Kiev now controlled all former Soviet military units in Ukraine, specifically including their tactical nuclear weapons. Zhivitsa went out of his way to emphasize that despite the impression created by the agreement, only the strategic weapons in Ukraine, and not the tactical weapons, would be controlled by the Combined Strategic Forces Command.[22] And although Zhivitsa reiterated that

---

[19]*International Herald Tribune*, December 21–22, 1991.

[20]*Pravda*, December 23, 1991.

[21]TASS, December 31, 1991. Kravchuk later remarked that it was agreed that the presidents of the four nuclear republics would obtain special telephone equipment with which to conduct a conference call if a nuclear decision were required.

[22]RFE/RL Daily Report, January 17, 1992. Thus, Zhivitsa's statement would appear to imply that because of what was happening to the general-purpose ground forces of the former Soviet Union, some proliferation of nuclear control had already occurred, if only temporarily.

the tactical weapons would all be removed from Ukraine by July 1, 1992, even this promise was to be temporarily placed in doubt in March, when Ukrainian President Kravchuk announced a halt to these transfers. Eventually, however, Kravchuk was to retreat under Western pressure, and the movement of the tactical warheads to Russia was at length resumed and completed.

THE IMPASSE OVER JOINT ARMED FORCES

The new agreement published on the last day of the year by the twelve republics now comprising the new Commonwealth had specified that the Combined Strategic Forces Command to be headed by Shaposhnikov would control not only strategic weapons systems but also the air force, navy, and air defense commands, the space command, the airborne troops, and military intelligence. Even these provisions, as will be seen, were ambiguous and soon became a matter of dispute. At the same time, a parallel attempt to transform Soviet general-purposes forces into joint Commonwealth forces was crippled when Ukraine and a few other republics refused and insisted on setting up their own armed forces from the Soviet forces stationed on their territory.

Within the next few weeks, as Ukraine pressed the issue of the allegiance of the hundreds of thousands of general-purpose ground troops on its soil, it apparently won over the bulk of the local command structure and the General Staff lost communications with these units in Ukraine. Meanwhile, the ambiguities in the December understanding about the Combined Strategic Forces Command also came to the surface, since a protracted dispute now emerged between Ukraine and Russia over the definition of "strategic forces," a term that the General Staff had long used very broadly. In particular, considerable mutual animosity soon developed over the issue of which units of the Black Sea Fleet would fall into this categtory, and remain with the Commonwealth, and which should be considered general-purpose ships and be taken over by Ukraine.

In sum, by the close of 1991, large gaps had suddenly appeared in the traditional all-union military structure, while the remaining parts of that structure were now functioning in the name of the Commonwealth but were generally seen as Russian in all but name. Meanwhile, cases of indiscipline by far-flung local commanders were multiplying, as supplies and funds to support the military machinery dwindled. Unable to bear the accustomed burden any longer because of the economic crisis, Russia prepared for a much more rapid contraction of the armed forces inherited from the union than Shaposhnikov had envisaged. The question of how far and how long Russia would continue to maintain an extraterritorial military presence in the non-Russian republics under the banner of the Commonwealth remained unclear, and the answer would henceforth be dependent on the development of Russia's political and economic dealings with each of the republics.

THE FUTURE OF DEFENSE DECISIONMAKING INSTITUTIONS

Under these circumstances, the nature of future decisionmaking political-military organs would also necessarily await the evolution of political events. The old all-union bodies such as the VPK, the Defense Council, and the President's Group on Negotiations had died with the Soviet state, if not before. In the republics that had begun to form their own armies, notably Ukraine and Azerbaydzhan, legislation by the turn of the year had created republic defense councils basically on the old model, albeit with some new variations.[23] In Russia, however, the problem was not so simple.

In Moscow, the building of such new institutions was at first delayed in early 1992 by the felt need to maintain the Commonwealth military facade. There were a variety of reasons why many different quarters wanted to postpone the disappearance of this facade. The West saw it as essential to prevent the proliferation of control over the nuclear assets of the former Soviet Union. Kazakhstan President Nazarbayev saw the Commonwealth as needed to contain the internal demographic pressures (of Russians versus Kazakhs) that might otherwise tear his republic apart.

For their part, the Russian generals who commanded the Commonwealth military organization considered it indispensable for a transitional period to bridge the gap until more permanent understandings could be reached between Russia and other republics regarding the status of the forces and weaponry of the former Soviet Union deployed outside Russia.[24] The Russian military leaders worried about the effect on other republics if, in the absence of such

---

[23]Ukraine broke new ground by including leaders of key legislative committees in its defense council.

[24]Radio Moscow reported on February 7, 1992, that the Commonwealth military command had in fact already developed a tentative plan for dividing up the general-purpose forces of the former Soviet Union. According to this plan, two-thirds of the ground forces, including armor and artillery, and two-thirds of aviation would go to Russia, with the rest distributed among the other Commonwealth states. This was not acceptable to the other republics. (RFE/RL Daily Report, No. 27, February 10, 1992.)

agreements, Russia took formal control of the forces nominally subordinated to the Commonwealth. Shaposhnikov and his colleagues feared that without the Commonwealth there would be an acceleration of the tendency of republics to take the Ukrainian path, creating armies of their own and advancing unilateral claims to the weapons and soldiers stationed on their soil. They were all the more convinced of this danger because the provisions for conventional weapons reduction contained in the CFE treaty had already forced the ex-Soviet republics west of the Urals to confront the issue of sharing out the inherited Soviet weaponry, and because these discussions had reached an impasse.

On the other hand, many democrats in Moscow were alarmed at what they regarded as the dangerous lack of subordination of the heirs of the old Soviet military establishment to the Russian state and to popular control. At the same time, many in the army shared great unease over the army's lack of formal subordination to a state, the lack of a clear mission and doctrine, and the absence of a formal structure linking it to the political leadership.

This dilemma was compounded by the fact that Yeltsin and Shaposhnikov also found it impossible to create Commonwealth decisionmaking organs analogous to the old Defense Council because of the widespread reluctance of other republics to revive the apparatus of a new central state. As usual, Ukraine was most outspoken in this respect, as President Kravchuk repeatedly made clear his view that the Commonwealth was at most a transitional and ephemeral institution, the already marginal need for which, in his opinion, would evaporate completely with the removal of the last nuclear weapons from Ukraine by 1994. But even republics that wanted to maintain a long-term military connection with Russia were reluctant to agree to create an administrative superstructure for that purpose. Only with difficulty were the republics persuaded to establish even a small Commonwealth secretariat to function in Minsk and provide continuity between the occasional meetings of the republic heads of state and heads of government. And while the political headquarters of the Commonwealth had been fixed in Belarus to minimize anxieties about Russian domination, the situation in the military sphere was necessarily more awkward politically, since the massive General Staff facilities and nerve center in Moscow could hardly be moved elsewhere.

In the first weeks of the Commonwealth's existence, little was accomplished to resolve this impasse, and there was little early evidence of the functioning of institutional mechanisms for political-military coordination at either the Commonwealth or the purely Russian level. Thus, early in the year Yeltsin suffered some embarrassment over repercussions of a December missile firing from Kazakhstan which, among other things, had evidently not been disclosed in advance to the Kazakh government.[25] A few weeks later, when Yeltsin visited the United Nations and the United States and made a variety of strategic announcements and proposals, there were reports of concern in Moscow that some of his suggestions had not been systematically staffed and coordinated.[26] Moreover, Yeltsin put forward his UN proposals frankly on behalf of Russia, ignoring the Commonwealth, which in the December Declaration had ostensibly been given control of the nuclear weapons he was now offering to reduce. This behavior evoked repeated subsequent protests from the Kazakh government, which complained that he had not, in fact, coordinated his proposals with Alma-Ata.[27] Nazarbayev warned that the West should understand the Yeltsin did not speak for Kazakhstan on nuclear disarmament matters,[28] and he insisted that disarmament issues should be resolved through consultations with military experts and in coordination with "all" Commonwealth states.[29]

These institutional anomalies impelled the Russian government toward making difficult institutional choices. On the strategic side, Yeltsin moved after the fact to attempt to coordinate his various recent strategic proposals at a new Minsk meeting of Commonwealth heads of state on February 14. At the same time, he sought to seize the occasion to obtain agreement "to vest the supreme coordinating military functions" with the Council of the Commonwealth Heads of State.[30] Despite the refusal of Ukraine, Azerbaydzhan, and Moldova to participate in a Commonwealth army, the February meeting decided to formalize an umbrella structure for this purpose, with Shaposhnikov as commander, and to appoint three deputies under

---

[25]*Izvestiya.* January 21, 1992.

[26]In late January 1992, the military industrial leader Viktor Surikov confirmed privately that the arms control decisionmaking system had broken down. (Gottemoeller and Aldrin.) However, Shaposhnikov publicly supported the Yeltsin proposals, suggesting that he, at least, had privately discussed them with Yeltsin.

[27]*Interfax* (Moscow), January 31, 1992 (FBIS-SOV, January 31, 1992, p. 4.) It would appear that whether or not the Kazakhs were informed in advance of what Yeltsin intended to say, they were not given a role in helping to devise the proposals.

[28]Interview with *Die Presse* (Vienna), February 6, 1992.

[29]*Interfax* (Moscow), February 5, 1992, reporting Nazarbayev statements alleged to have been made to a visiting German official. (RFE/RL Daily Report, No. 25, February 6, 1992.)

[30]TASS, January 22, 1992.

him to serve as chief of staff and to direct the strategic forces and the general-purpose forces.[31]

This arrangement, however, remained fragile and inadequate because it did not address the craving in the army for a much more coherent military structure than the Commonwealth is likely to permit. In March, Yeltsin took a small step in that direction when he at last announced the creation of a Russian Ministry of Defense, headed, temporarily, by himself. Initially, the ministry was not yet given any functions, and Yeltsin sidestepped the issue of a Russian army by assuming control of the forces actually controlled by the CIS and simultaneously redesignating them back to CIS control. Meanwhile, however, Russia had edged closer to the Rubicon: the negotiation of bilateral or multilateral mutual security or status of forces agreements between Russia and other republics that would define the terms under which Russian troops would in future years remain deployed outside Russia. The conclusion of such agreements would presumably be accompanied by the negotiation of agreements parcelling out the conventional weaponry of the former Soviet Union among the republics. When and if these understandings are finally reached, Russia's need for a Commonwealth title for its general-purpose forces may recede, although the requirement for a CIS umbrella for strategic forces may endure much longer.

In the meantime, the emergence of the Russian Ministry of Defense brought to the surface a heated political struggle in Moscow over the future structure and orientation of the Russian military establishment and the organizations that will control it. In the spring of 1992, many civilian and military reformers were greatly concerned at the scant changes that had been made in this establishment since the August 1991 coup, and sought to use the occasion of the creation of the ministry to seize control of the high command, to purge it and reconstruct it. A fierce dispute was in progress over this question.

One of the issues involved in this ongoing struggle will inevitably be the identity and ideological orientation of the actors involved in whatever new supreme institutions for national security coordinating and decisionmaking eventually reemerge in Russia. In the late spring of 1992, a step was taken toward resolution of this issue when legislation was enacted creating a Russian Federation Security Council. Designed to make policy on issues of broadly defined domestic as well as foreign security, the new Russian Security Council evidently drew

---

[31]*Los Angeles Times,* February 15, 1992. Uzbekistan and Belarus agreed to participate only during a two-year transitional period.

much of its inspiration from the plan for a USSR Security and Defense Council unsuccessfully urged upon Gorbachev by Velikhov in February 1990, as described earlier in this report. Chaired by Yeltsin as president, the Russian Security Council would have four other ex officio permanent members: Vice President Aleksandr Rutskoy, the first deputy chairman of the Supreme Soviet, the chairman of the Council of Ministers, and a Security Council secretary to be appointed by Yeltsin. In addition, Yeltsin was apparently given discretion to nominate to the Council any of ten designated ministers, half of whom were concerned with domestic rather than foreign policy matters. Other leaders could attend sessions on an *ad hoc* basis as "consultants."[32]

Thus, despite the fact that Yeltsin soon named a professional soldier—Army General Pavel Grachev—to succeed himself as Minister of Defense, rather than the civilian minister sought by many Russian democrats, the democrats could take some comfort from the nature of the decisionmaking organ created to supervise Grachev. They could hope—much as Velikhov had hoped in 1990—that a barrier had been created to the resurrection of General Staff control of the Council. With the Russian Security Council charged with considering security matters in such a broad sense, the General Staff could not appropriately serve as the secretariat for the Council's nonmilitary work.

Nevertheless, the key question of the nature of the supporting apparatus for the Defense Council remained to be determined, and here, unfortunately, Russia still has before it the ill-fated model of the network that supported the defense councils of the past in the Central Committee departments and the presidential office. The military-industrial expert Viktor Surikov in late January 1992 painted a picture of numerous functionaries of the old decisionmaking structure waiting to be called back to action by the resuscitation of that structure.[33] A month earlier, a TASS report had asserted that Yeltsin was well aware of the "highly-qualified specialists" who had served in the defense department of Gorbachev's presidential staff, and alleged that "nearly all the department's staff" would switch to work for Yeltsin once Russia established a Ministry of Defense.[34]

---

[32]*Rossiyskaya Gazeta*, May 6, 1992 (FBIS-SOV, May 6, 1992, pp. 37–38). One of the important innovations in this legislation was the designation of a permanent role for a representative of the Russian Parliament in security policymaking. As earlier noted, Ukraine had already taken a similar step in setting up its own Defense Council.

[33]Gottemoeller and Aldrin.

[34]TASS, December 25, 1991 (FBIS-SOV, December 26, 1991, p. 41).

Unfortunately, however, we have seen that the presidential department in question had been staffed in large part with officials recruited from the CPSU Central Committee Military Department, and had been led by the intransigent defense industry apparatchik and coup conspirator Oleg Baklanov. Thus, many of those who had the expertise required for support of military-political decisionmaking had acquired their career experience through long association with some of the more reactionary institutions and personalities of the old Soviet regime. The possibility that such individuals could return—and could eventually seek to revive the attitudes of the past—is underlined by the continued survival of reactionary veterans of the Soviet period in other Russian institutions, notably the successor organization to the KGB. The direction taken in future years by any new Russian national security decisionmaking organ may therefore be heavily influenced by the personnel choices made by Yeltsin at the outset. The long-term importance of this issue was further underscored in the spring of 1992 by disturbing signs that Yeltsin was coming under increasing pressure to make concessions to the traditionally dominant forces in the military institution.